INSIDE OUT

Book by
DOUG HAVERTY
Music by
ADRYAN RUSS
Lyrics by
ADRYAN RUSS
& DOUG HAVERTY

D1789414

S A M U E L   F R E N C H ,   I N C .
45 West 25th Street   NEW YORK 10010
7623 Sunset Boulevard   HOLLYWOOD 90046
LONDON   *TORONTO*

IMPORTANT
BILLING AND CREDIT REQUIREMENTS

All producers of INSIDE OUT *must* give credit to the Creators of the Work in all programs distributed in connection with performances of the Work and in all instances in which the title of the Work appears for the purposes of advertising, publicizing, or otherwise exploiting the Work and/or a production. The names of the Creators *must* also appear on a separate line, one which no other name appears, immediately following the title, and *must* appear in size of type not less than fifty percent the size of the title type. Billing *must* be substantially as follows:

(Name of Producer)
presents

INSIDE OUT

Book by	Music by	Lyrics by
DOUG HAVERTY	ADRYAN RUSS	ADRYAN RUSS & DOUG HAVERTY

In addition: The following *must* appear wherever and whenever the above mentioned Creators' names appear.

Original New York Production directed by Henry Fonte
and choreographed by Gary Slavin.

With regard to Henry Fonte's credit, his first and last name may not be less than 40% of the size of the largest letter used for the title of the play (Exclusive of art titles) or the names of the stars, in any, whichever is larger but under no circumstances not less than 100% of the same size, type and prominence as the Creators' billing.

INSIDE OUT opened November 7, 1994 at the Cherry Lane Theatre, New York, NY. Produced by: Marc Routh, Richard Frankel, Randy Kelly, Carol Ostrow, George Tunick, Margot Ross London & Prima K. Stephen. Directed by Henry Fonte. Choreography by Gary Slavin. Orchestrations by Ned Ginsburg. Musical Direction & Vocal Arrangements by E. Suzan Ott. Scenery by Rob Odorisio. Costumes by Gail Brassard. Lighting by Douglas O'Flaherty. Casting by Alan Filderman.

CAST:

Dena	ANN CRUMB
Grace	HARRIETT D. FOY
Molly	KATHLEEN MAHONY-BENNETT
Liz	JAN MAXWELL
Chlo	CASS MORGAN
Sage	JULIE PROSSER

Alternates: Leah Hocking, Lisby Larson, Jennifer Naimo & Maureen Silliman.

INSIDE OUT originally opened (under the title "Roleplay") on April 27, 1989 at The Group Repertory Theatre, North Hollywood, CA. Produced by Lonny Chapman and Robert Schanche. Directed by Allison R. Liddi. Musical numbers staged by Pat Carney. Lighting by Keith Endo. Scenery by Caulder Atkins. Musical Conductor & Arrangements by Carol Weiss. Costumes by Shari L. Nigel.

CAST:

Dena	JULIE BLOOMFIELD
Molly	JODI CARLISLE
Chlo	CLAUDIA FENTON
Liz	PAT LENTZ
Sage	REENIE MOORE
Grace	BONNIE SNYDER

Alternates: Christy Barrett, Carole Chene, Sonja Fortag, Eileen Johnson & Pamela Brewbaker.

CAST
(In Order of Appearance.)

DENA:

(30's - 40's) Attractive, bitter, singer/actress, currently divorced and living alone. Her briefly successful career has stalled and she is searching for an explanation. She senses that she is the cause of her predicament, but cannot admit it.

GRACE:

(40's - 50's) Intelligent, sensitive, easy-going, centered, "graceful" group therapy leader. She has a sense of humor and loves what she's doing. She is happily married.

SAGE:

(30's) Genuinely sincere, deeply caring, naive woman who would have been a hippie if she'd been born at the right time. She is almost engaged.

CHLO:

(30's) Beautiful, feminine, sarcastic, loving, gay mother with a troublesome 14-year-old son. She is a therapy pro, romantically alone, an artist who sketches during group.

MOLLY:

(30's) Cute, self-doubting, paranoid, happily-married new mother who's convinced she waited too long to have children and will never lose her maternity weight even though she has.

LIZ:

(30's - 40's) Striking, confident, driven, professional executive who has fought her way up a corporate ladder while managing to support a house-husband and three teenage children. She has a hard time determining which comes first: career or family.

SCENE

The story takes place in a large metropolitan city in the U.S.A., maybe New York. The time is the not-too-distant-past. The action is continuous.

SETTING

The set should be a unit set.

There should be six chairs in a semi-circle, perhaps on a revolve so they always come to us from a different angle, or the chairs could be on wheels.

The set should have an open, imaginative feeling and not be confining.

MUSICAL NUMBERS

ACT ONE:

"Inside Out" . . . . COMPANY

"Let It Go" . . . . SAGE & GRACE

"Thin" . . . . MOLLY & COMPANY

"I Can See You Here" . . . . GRACE

"If You Really Loved Me . . . . COMPANY

"Yo, Chlo" . . . . DENA & CHLO

"If You Really Loved Me" *(Reprise)* . . . . CHLO

"Behind Dena's Back" . . . . COMPANY

"No One Inside" . . . . DENA

"Inside Out" *(Reprise)* . . . . COMPANY

ACT TWO:

"Grace's Nightmare" . . . . GRACE & COMPANY

"All I Do Is Sing" . . . . DENA

"Never Enough" . . . . CHLO

"I Don't Say Anything" . . . . SAGE

"The Passing Of A Friend" . . . MOLLY & COMPANY

"Things Look Different" . . . . LIZ & COMPANY

"Do It At Home" . . . . LIZ & COMPANY

"Reaching Up" . . . . DENA & COMPANY

ACT ONE

SONG: "INSIDE OUT" *(COMPANY)*

LIZ:
I GOTTA GO.
GRACE:
I GOTTA GO.
DENA:
I GOTTA GO.
SAGE:
I GOTTA GO.
CHLO:
I GOTTA GO.
MOLLY:
I GOTTA GO.
CHLO, LIZ, MOLLY & SAGE:
I GOTTA GO,
I BETTER RUN,
I HAVE FORTY THINGS TO DO
BEFORE THE DAY IS DONE.
I MAKE A CALL,
I WRITE A CHECK,
BEFORE I KNOW WHAT HIT ME,
I'M A TOTAL WRECK.

I START TO SWEAT,
MY SKIN TURNS GRAY,
THEN I SUDDENLY REMEMBER
I HAVE GROUP TODAY.
SOME TIME FOR ME,
BE STILL, MY HEART,
I HOPE IT GETS HERE SOON
BEFORE I FALL APART.
GRACE:
FIND A WAY IN,

OPEN A DOOR
WALK THROUGH YOUR MIRROR OF DOUBT,
GO PAST THE SKIN,
RIGHT TO THE CORE,
WHERE ALL YOUR HOPES HIDE OUT.
TURN THE INSIDE OUT.

    CHLO:
WHY GO TO GROUP?
IT'S WHAT I FEARED.
NO MATTER WHAT I TELL THEM
THEY WILL THINK I'M WEIRD.

    MOLLY:
WHY OPEN UP?
WHY CRACK THE VAULT?
IT'S CLEAR THAT WHO I AM
IS ALL MY MOTHER'S FAULT.

    LIZ:
WHY JOIN A GROUP?
FOR SMILES AND YUKS?
I COULD STAY AT HOME AND CRY
AND SAVE A HUNDRED BUCKS.

    SAGE:
DO I NEED HELP?
AM I A KLUTZ?
OR IS THE WORLD IN SUCH A MESS
WE'RE ALL A LITTLE NUTS?

(The following parts are sung simultaneously, as indicated.)

GRACE:	**COMPANY:**
FIND A WAY IN,	WHY DO I DO THAT?
OPEN A DOOR,	WHY DID YOU LET ME?
WHAT ARE YOUR FENCES ...	CAN I CLIMB OVER ...
ABOUT?	THE WALL AROUND
	MY HEART?

    ALL:
NO MORE ESCAPES,
SCRAP THE CHARADES.

GRACE:
AREN'T YOU ALL LIED OUT?
ALL:
ALL CRIED OUT.
GRACE:
TURN THE INSIDE OUT.

(In an imaginary mirror, DENA is trying on various outfits.)

DENA:
WHY JOIN A GROUP?
WHY SUFFER PAIN?
WHY WALK IN A ROOM ON PURPOSE
WHERE THEY'RE ALL INSANE?
I'M INSECURE, SO WHAT'S THE CRIME? THERE.
I'VE DIAGNOSED MYSELF IN HALF THE TIME.
LIZ:
THE MEETING'S OFF?
I CANNOT WAIT!
FAX THE AD TOMORROW MORNING,
I CANNOT BE LATE.
SAGE:
THE HOMELESS PEOPLE SAID
THE FOOD I MADE WAS STALE.
HOW CAN YOU
DO CHARITY AND FAIL?
LIZ:
HOW CAN YOU DO IT AND FAIL?

MOLLY:	**SAGE & LIZ:**
THE BABY'S WET,	LA LA LA LA
I LOOK A FRIGHT,	LA LA LA LA
TWENTY PEOPLE EATING	LA LA LA LA
DINNER	LA LA LA LA
AT MY HOUSE TONIGHT.	HA! HA!

CHLO:	**SAGE, LIZ & MOLLY:**
WISH I WERE HOME,	AH
AND WITH MY SON,	AH

INSTEAD OF TRYING
   TO MAKE
THIS GODDAM OFFICE RUN.
   DENA:
HELLO, MY NAME IS DENA ...
AND I'M A LITTLE NERVOUS ... NO!
WHY JOIN A GROUP?
LIFE IS TOO SHORT,
I COULD BUY PANTYHOSE
AND SURELY GET AS MUCH SUPPORT.
   ALL:
I CANNOT THINK,
MY BRAIN IS FRIED.
I NEED TO SEE A SHRINK
AND TAKE A LOOK INSIDE ... LOOK INSIDE.

GRACE:	**DENA:**
FIND A WAY IN,	NOTHING TO LOSE,
OPEN A DOOR.	I'M NOT GONNA DIE.
WALK THROUGH	
YOUR DOUBT	I WILL
GIVE IT A TRY.	GIVE IT A TRY.

   GRACE & DENA:
GIVE IT A TRY.
   LIZ, MOLLY, GRACE
   & SAGE:

A PLACE TO ESCAPE,	
AWAY FROM THE CROWD.	**DENA:**
BE GOOD TO MYSELF,	BE GOOD TO MYSELF,
IT'S ALLOWED.	IT'S ALLOWED.
ROLL UP THE SHADES.	HOW AM I GONNA
	SURVIVE?
NO MORE CHARADES.	HOW CAN I FEEL
	MORE ALIVE?

I'M FULL OF DOUBT,
   ALL:
WHAT'S IT ABOUT?
I'M GOING, I'M GOING, I'M GOING TO GROUP
TO TURN THE INSIDE OUT!

(GRACE has arranged the chairs. LIGHTS UP with everyone seated except DENA.)

LIZ: Grace, are you sure she's coming or is she just unfashionably nine minutes late?

MOLLY: She's probably like me. The hardest part about going to a group the first day is deciding what to wear.

SAGE: Dena: I-N-A or E-N-A? I have to do her numbers.

LIZ, CHLO, MOLLY & GRACE: 'E!'

SAGE: Oh. *(Beat)* 'K.

GRACE: Let's show Dena a productive, meaningful, juicy session.

CHLO: Oh, a blast from the past? Let's see, do we remember what we all said during Liz's ordeal about separate vacations from the kids?

LIZ: Why do you always bring that up?

CHLO: God. Do you realize,we've been together so long, I've forgotten what everyone's *initial* madness was.

SAGE: Yeah, when I came in, I was so messed up I blanked out on most of your problems. Now that I'm slightly better, I can be more receptive to your shit.

MOLLY: Can we change seats?

LIZ: Why?

MOLLY: I don't want to sit next to Dena and have her see my thighs squashing out of the third dimension.

GRACE: Sure.

(They ALL change seats as DENA, wearing severe sunglasses, enters and watches.)

DENA: Hi. I'm Dena White and ... I'm ...

LIZ: Late.

GRACE: Welcome! This is Chlo, Molly, Liz & Sage.

ALL: *(Awkward and discordant)* Hi.

(DENA sits down and looks around the group. They ALL stare at her. ALL sit in silence for a few beats.)

SAGE: *(To DENA)* God, I really love your garb. And I admire you for having the courage to wear it.

MOLLY: I swear my four-year-old has a Barbie outfit just like that.

LIZ: *(To DENA)* You've gone in for a new look, I see.

DENA: Several. Sometimes at the same time.

CHLO: I think I have all your records and –

MOLLY: Me, too. Well, I mean my husband does.

CHLO: I haven't listened – my 14-year-old son monopolizes the stereo.

SAGE: *(To DENA)* You're an "eight"? "Destined for fame and immense wealth." *(To others)* I've never met a *real* "eight." Wow.

(DENA nods slowly. SLIGHT PAUSE.)

GRACE: Why doesn't everyone tell Dena what they do?

CHLO: We're professional group therapy-ettes.

LIZ: Speak for yourself. Liz Rogers, Vice-President of Marketing at Nadine-Ness Cosmetics.

SAGE: I'm Sage and I work at Dutton Books and I make custom-made bookmarks. I sell and order.

MOLLY: Dena White, Molly Gorman. I'm an ex-buyer of stationery and notions for J.C. Penney; now a *more* than full-time housewife and career-mother. Ecch. That sounds so self-deprecating, doesn't it? *(Beat)* I'm doing that. I should shut up.

CHLO: Chlo. I'm in personnel at CitiBank. I sketch and sculpt on the side to retain my humanity. *(To GRACE)* Now shall we tell Dena our most embarrassing moments?

LIZ: Chlo, your whole life's been one, long, embarrassing moment.

CHLO: So has yours only no one's had the nerve to tell you.

SAGE: Come on, you guys. You're putting negative vibrations out. That's not good on Dena's first day.

GRACE: Right. Let's work. Who's first? *(Beat) Who* wants to work? I know you're all anxious to. *(Beat)* What about you, Sage?

SAGE: Me?

GRACE: Yes. Do you have something to report to the group?

SAGE: Oh, yeah. I kinda, sorta went to Grace's house.

DENA: I thought we weren't supposed to do that.

LIZ: We're not.

MOLLY: But we do.

GRACE: *But we're not supposed to!*

SAGE: Right.

GRACE: And when we do, we ... ?

(She looks to SAGE to finish the sentence.)

SAGE: We show the group. But Grace, I can't show them me, standing there at your door, saying nothing while staring at your gorgeous husband – *(To others)* who was only wearing running shorts.

GRACE: Let's pick up from where you remembered spoken language.

(SAGE stands up and crosses to GRACE.)

SAGE: Forget I was here.

GRACE: How can I? You walked in without an appointment, permeated the air with patchouli, interrupted a crucial argument about the theme of my new book. Talk!

SAGE: It's Garth.

GRACE: Garth?

SAGE: Yeah. He's that book salesman I met on the "End Hunger" walk. We've been out three times now.

GRACE: Good!

SAGE: And he wants to go a fourth round.

GRACE: Excellent!

SAGE: Grace, I've never made it past a third date.

GRACE: Hasn't that always been your decision?

SAGE: Yes. I just subconsciously blow the second and third dates.

LIZ, CHLO & MOLLY: Sage!

GRACE: And this time you didn't?

SAGE: I tried! *(Beat)* But he liked everything I did. I'm terrified.

GRACE: Of what? *(MUSIC BEGINS)* That this might be right?

SONG: "LET IT GO" *(GRACE & SAGE)*

SAGE:
DON'T SAY THAT. IT CAN'T.
THE STARS ARE ALL WRONG.
I'VE HAD MY CARDS READ EVERY DAY THIS WEEK.
AND THE FORECAST LOOKS POSITIVELY BLEAK.

EVERY TIME MY HEART SAYS, "GREAT!"
THE CARDS SAY, "WAIT!"
EVERY TIME MY HEART SAYS, "RIGHT!"
THE STARS SAY, "NOT QUITE."
EVERY TIME I'D SWEAR I HAD IT MADE,
MERCURY GOES INTO RETROGRADE.
EVERY TIME MY GUT SAYS, "GO!"
THE CARDS SAY, "NO."
    GRACE:
DID THE CARDS ACTUALLY SAY, "HE'S NO GOOD"?
    SAGE: *(Spoken)* Well, not exactly.
    GRACE:
HAVE THEY SAID, "GARTH IS NOT THE MAN FOR YOU?"
    SAGE: *(Spoken)* Well, no, they didn't.
    GRACE:
HAVE THEY TAUGHT YOU THE TRUTH INSIDE YOUR
    HEART?
    SAGE: *(Spoken)* They can't do that.
    GRACE:
WELL, I KNOW HOW TO START.
EVERY TIME YOUR HEART SAYS, "YO!"
LET IT GO!
    SAGE: *(Spoken)* What?
    GRACE:
EVERY TIME YOUR HEART SAYS, "AI!"

LET IT FLY!

    SAGE: *(Spoken)* But –

    GRACE:

DON'T SAY THE CARDS ARE NEVER WRONG,

HOW DO YOU KNOW FOR SURE?

COME ON DOWN FROM THE SKIES,

CLEAR THE FOG FROM YOUR EYES,

PUT YOUR FEET ON THE GROUND,

TAKE A GOOD LOOK AROUND,

WHEN YOUR HEART SAYS, "HAPPINESS!"

TELL IT, "YES!"

    SAGE:

YES?

    GRACE:

YES!

    SAGE:

YES!

    GRACE:

EVERY TIME YOUR HEART SAYS, "YO!"

    SAGE:

LET IT GO!

    GRACE:

LET IT GO!

EVERY TIME YOUR HEART SAYS, "AI!"

    SAGE:

LET IT FLY!

    GRACE:

LET IT FLY!

    GRACE & SAGE:

DON'T SAY THE CARDS ARE NEVER WRONG,

HOW DO YOU KNOW FOR SURE?

    GRACE:

COME ON DOWN FROM THE SKIES,

    SAGE:

CLEAR THE FOG FROM MY EYES,

    GRACE:

PUT YOUR FEET ON THE GROUND.

SAGE:
TAKE A GOOD LOOK AROUND.
　　GRACE & SAGE:
WHEN YOUR HEART SAYS, "HAPPINESS!"
　　GRACE:
TELL IT, "YES!"
　　SAGE:
YES.
　　GRACE:
GOODBYE.
　　SAGE:
GOODBYE?
　　GRACE:
EVERY TIME YOUR HEART SAYS, "YO!"
　　SAGE:
LET IT GO.
　　GRACE:
(As she pushes SAGE out the door she sings)
GO.
　　SAGE:
GO!
　　GRACE:
GO!
　　GRACE & SAGE:
GO!

(GRACE pushes SAGE out the door and slumps.)

　　LIZ: Sage, that's wonderful. So, Grace convinced you to toss your cards?

　　SAGE: No, but I'm listening to my heart more. And now, every time my *heart* says, "happiness," I do the cards for *it.*

　　LIZ: What?

　　SAGE: I'm treating my heart as a separate entity. Even though it's part of Sage, it's another ray of my light; a whole 'nother energy source.

　　LIZ: Of course.

　　GRACE: All right, who's next?

MOLLY: *(Beat)* Grace, don't look at me.

GRACE: I'm looking at everyone.

MOLLY: But you're looking hardest into me and I spilled strained apricots on my top and nothing else was clean because all I wash is diapers and I can't go next. *(Beat)* Oh. I guess I kinda already have, huh?

LIZ: *What* are you thinking about working on *today*?

MOLLY: Last night, Harry made me ... go off my diet.

CHLO: And now you're back on it?

(MUSIC BEGINS.)

MOLLY: Yeah. But I feel ... I'm not ... Oh,

SONG: "THIN" *(MOLLY & COMPANY)*

MOLLY:
GOSH, I LOVED BEING PREGNANT
FOOD WAS NEVER TABOO
YOU COULD EAT LIKE A HORSE
AND JUST SMILE AND SAY,
"HEY! I'M EATING FOR TWO."
AFTER THE BABY YOU'RE FULL OF EXCUSES
YOU TRY LIKE THE DEVIL TO FIGHT 'EM:
"THERE'S NO TIME FOR EXERCISE,"
"I'M HEALING, YOU REALIZE,"
"MY BODY MUST STABILIZE ..."
AND ON AND ON AD INFINITUM.

BUT THE BABY IS ALMOST ONE
AND THIS BARREL IS NO LONGER FUN.
EVERY DAY I GET DEPRESSED
'CAUSE BENEATH THIS LIQUID ARMOR
THERE'S A TWIGGY WHO'S SUPPRESSED.

THIN,
I WANT TO BE THIN
I WANT TO BE IN THE MOVIES KIND OF

INDISPUTABLY THIN
LIKE I'VE NEVER BEEN
I'VE GOT TOO MUCH SKIN
TO MAKE THIS MAXI-MINI.
I WANNA WEAR SKINNY CLOTHES
MADE OF SILK AND SATIN,
MANHATTAN CLOTHES
I WANT TO LOOK HOT
NOT FAT IN.
THIN,
I IDOLIZE THIN
BUT FANTASIZE SINFUL RECIPES ...
THAT INCONTROLLABLY WIN.
IF I COULD JUST NOT GIVE IN
I COULD BE REALLY THIN.

MY DRESSES ARE TIGHT
MY BLUE JEANS ARE A RIOT,
I SWEAR EVERY NIGHT
TOMORROW I START MY DIET
BUT NEXT DAY I DENY IT!
    LIZ, CHLO & SAGE:
THIN
I WANT TO BE THIN
WHERE DO I BEGIN
TO WARD OFF THE WHIPPED CREAM PIES?
    MOLLY:
MAKE ME LESS OF A GLUTTON
MAKE MY LEVI'S BUTTON
    ALL:
HOW DO I BE A MIA FARROW?
    MOLLY:
NARROW AND NEAT AS A PIN.

                  OTHERS:
I WANT TO BE FRAIL   FRAIL, FRAIL
A PROVERBIAL RAIL   PROVERBIAL RAIL
    ALL:
MAKE MY BODY TAPER
UNTIL I'M PAPER THIN.

LIZ: Molly, do you feel thinner having stated your case ... again?

MOLLY: A smidgen. I probably just burned off twelve calories and that's the equivalent to a shaving from a chocolate-covered Swiss almond with a trace of Haagen-Daz still clinging to it. This pig is clamming up!

(She makes an "oink oink" noise.)

LIZ: Grace, you haven't asked Dena what her objectives are.

CHLO: That's because she knew you would.

DENA: I just came to observe.

LIZ: Huh uh. No way. I'm not going to start unloading until I at least know the basic parameters of your neurosis.

CHLO: Well, how unthinkable! To realize that we've gathered here with incomplete information.

LIZ: Shut up, Chlo.

CHLO: Why are you doing this?

LIZ: Can't you see that's what she needs?

CHLO: No. Oddly enough, I don't know what she needs. I don't think anyone does and you're being an asshole.

LIZ: I'm just trying to move things along.

GRACE: And you have.

DENA: *(Beat. Notices everyone is staring at her)* Everything's stale. I can't even stand to speak to my producer, agents, manager ... mother.

MOLLY: Me, too – Only, mother, I mean. I don't have an agent.

CHLO: We know, Mol.

DENA: My career's not exactly in the toilet, but let's say it's perched on the padded seat.

SAGE: *(To CHLO)* She's funny. I like her.

CHLO: Me, too.

DENA: And a friend said I wasn't making sense, that I should go see a shrink or join a group. And since I'm a singer, I liked the idea of trying a "group."

CHLO: How long ago was "Until Tonight"?

DENA: Eleven hitless years.

LIZ: And your homelife?

CHLO: *(To DENA)* Go ahead. Humor the parameter-queen.

DENA: I have one ... barely.

MOLLY: You were married to someone famous, weren't you?

DENA: David Resnick.

ALL: Oh, yeah.

LIZ: He did lots of commercials.

SAGE: And Celebrity Circus Specials!

MOLLY: And Soap Operas – not that I watch.

GRACE: How long were you married?

DENA: Legally, twenty-six months. Physically, seven.

CHLO: I remember when you got married. I was so disappointed.

DENA: Yeah. The jerk was a hunk.

CHLO: *(Beat)* No. I meant you.

DENA: Oh. I'm sorry. I'm usually better at –

CHLO: That's okay. My sexual signal indicator's a little rusty.

DENA: You have a son, right?

SAGE & MOLLY: Travis!

DENA: And you've been gay for – ?

CHLO: Ever.

DENA: Great.

CHLO: It's not ideal, but I don't regret it one minute.

LIZ: So what have you been doing about your career?

DENA: Making the rounds, climbing the walls.

SAGE: I'd love to help, but I don't follow music much. I listen, but it doesn't sink in. My last favorite song was, "Have You Never Been Mellow?" Remember that one?

GRACE: What active things have you done to promote yourself?

DENA: I'm looking for new management, agent, trying to write some of my own songs. I've never done that before. I want to change everything.

GRACE: Change can be good, right? Well, nice work, everyone. See you next week.

MOLLY: Where did the time go?

CHLO: It ran away with my youth.

(MOLLY and CHLO exit quickly.)

SAGE: *(As she exits)* Oh, my God. Are we done? Did I space?

LIZ: No. We started late. *(Calling off)* Chlo, wait up.

GRACE: *(To DENA)* I think you'd do very well here.

DENA: You do? Really?

GRACE: Yes.

(MUSIC BEGINS.)

DENA: I don't know. They're a tough crowd.

SONG: "I CAN SEE YOU HERE" *(GRACE)*

GRACE:
THERE'S NO CRYSTAL BALL
INSIDE MY HEAD
YET, I LOOK AT YOU,
AND THE TRUTH IS PLAIN.
TODAY I SAW YOU
FACING A NEW START,
ACHING TO FILL THIS ROOM
WITH THE MUSIC OF YOUR HEART.

I CAN SEE YOU HERE,
CLEAR AS I SEE YOUR FACE.
I CAN SEE YOU HERE,
SHOWING US WHO YOU ARE.
IF YOU TAKE THIS RISK,
AND FOLLOW THROUGH,
THERE'LL BE NO STOPPING YOU.

THE CHOICE IS YOURS
YOU CAN STOP YOUR FATE FROM TURNING,
WALK OUT THAT DOOR, FORGET THIS CHANCE.

THE CHOICE IS YOURS
YOU CAN OPEN YOURSELF TO LEARNING
A NEW SONG, A NEW DANCE.

I CAN SEE YOU HERE,
REACHING FOR SOMETHING NEW
YOU CAN BE YOU HERE,
SHOWING US ALL YOU'VE GOT.
IF YOU TAKE THIS RISK AND FOLLOW THROUGH
YOU'LL BE ON THE PATH
TO YOUR DREAM OF YOU.
I BELIEVE YOU CAN GET THERE,
I KNOW YOU KNOW HOW
START NOW
RIGHT HERE!

(DENA, moved by GRACE's encouragement, considers then exits.)

SONG: Scene Change 1

(LIGHT PATTERNS CHANGE. LIZ, MOLLY, CHLO & SAGE all RE-ENTER. GRACE re-positions the chairs.)

LIZ: In an effort to move things along, I'll tattle and say that Molly already started.
MOLLY: Did not.
LIZ: Did so.
MOLLY: Did – ! *(She stops)* Okay. I lied. I did, but –
CHLO: It was so embarrassing. There we were in the elevator and –
MOLLY: Chlo!
GRACE: Well, Molly, since you're warmed up, why don't you start?
MOLLY: No. That's okay. Chlo and I pretty much worked out my little problem.

(CHLO shakes her head "no.")

LIZ: Molly, spill.
MOLLY: Chlo! I didn't –
CHLO: You'll thank me, cutie.

(DENA enters and the tone shifts. She is late again and takes the empty chair.)

CHLO: Welcome back.
DENA: Thanks. Sorry I interrupted. I won't be late next time.
LIZ: Go on, Molly.
MOLLY: I can't. Someone else work.
GRACE: Why?
MOLLY: Sitting next to Dena I feel like a horror picture: "The Blob That Invaded Group!"
DENA: But you're not fat.
LIZ: Did you hear that? Does it mean more that it came from the mouth of a perfect stranger?
MOLLY: No.
DENA: *Where* are you fat?
MOLLY: Do you know a good liposuctionist?
LIZ: Go back to work.
MOLLY: I can't leave the kids.
CHLO: Don't you miss it?
MOLLY: I miss those business lunches. Especially the extravagantly expensive ones where you sit down with china, linen, flowers ... and adults. *(Beat)* But I wouldn't trade my peanut-butter and jelly on brown bread with a sticky glass of milk for all the tummy tucks in the world.
LIZ: Molly, I'm not buying this on-again-off-again anorexia nirvana. What's the real reason?
MOLLY: Oh, God. It's Harry. Who else? And it's sex. What else?
GRACE: Do you want to replay a specific instance with Harry?
MOLLY: No! No one here has the right "equipment" to play out the problems I'm having.
CHLO: Oh? *(Looks through her large purse)* Let me see what I brought today ... No, outta luck. *(Beat)* Molly, seriously,

take it from me; you're just as incredibly attractive now as you were before you had the babies.

MOLLY: That's what Harry says, too. But it's almost like he's covering up something. Five years ago, when you could still see ribs if I inhaled real deep, he never told me what a great body I had, he just took it. *(Beat)* Now, he says it, but doesn't ...

GRACE: What do you mean covering up?

MOLLY: I know, no big deal. Sex tapers off.

GRACE: Molly, your problem is very real to you and worth working on.

CHLO: Do you initiate?

MOLLY: Usually Harry's asleep and he works so hard. I hate to wake him to see if he wants ...

LIZ: Go to bed earlier.

GRACE: What do you think brought about this change in Harry?

MOLLY: I don't know. I get the feeling I don't feel good to Harry anymore. Like I'm all stretched out inside and it's not worth waiting up for. He services me if I wake him up, but I want him to want me. I want him to get up, carry me into the bedroom and take an hour caressing me before ... if he really loved me –

(MUSIC BEGINS.)

GRACE: He'd what? What would he do differently? Tell us exactly. In fact, I'll be Harry and you finish that sentence for me ten times.

SONG: "IF YOU REALLY LOVED ME" *(COMPANY)*

GRACE:
IF YOU REALLY LOVED ME, YOU WOULD ...
MOLLY:
MAKE LOVE ALL DAY
CHLO: *(Spoken)* Good one.
GRACE:
IF YOU REALLY LOVED ME, YOU WOULD ...
MOLLY:
SWEEP ME AWAY.

SAGE: *(Spoken)* Yeah.
MOLLY:
YOU WOULD BE ROMANTIC
BY A FIRE.
MAKE ME FRANTIC
WITH DESIRE.
WORK LESS, PLAY MORE.
NEVER PEE TIL YOU SHUT THE BATHROOM DOOR.

IF YOU REALLY LOVED ME ...
LIZ:
YOU WOULD CALL WHEN YOU'RE LATE.
GRACE:
IF YOU REALLY LOVED ME ...
MOLLY:
YOU WOULD HELP ME LOSE WEIGHT.
SAGE:
YOU'D REMEMBER MY BIRTHDAY,
CHLO:
SEND ME FLOWERS,
LIZ:
MAKE LOVE FASTER,
SAGE:
MAKE LOVE LAST FOR HOURS.
CHLO:
TALK MORE.
MOLLY:
TALK LESS.
LIZ:
WHEN I ASK FOR EVERYTHING, JUST SAY, "YES."
ALL:
YES!
LIZ:
OHHHH. IF YOU REALLY LOVED ME ...
GRACE:
YOU WOULD ALWAYS AGREE WITH ME,
MOLLY:
LOVE TO BE WITH ME.

CHLO:
TELL ME WHAT YOU'RE THINKING NOW AND THEN.
SAGE:
NEVER TELL ME POLISH JOKES AGAIN.

(GRACE pushes DENA up to try it.)

DENA:
IF YOU REALLY LOVED ME ...
GRACE:
YOU WOULD RUN WITH ME AT DAWN.
MOLLY: *(Spoken)* Yeah.
DENA:
IF YOU REALLY LOVED ME ...
CHLO:
YOU WOULD NEVER BE GONE.
LIZ:
YOU WOULD STOP YOUR SWEARING,
MOLLY:
DO LESS DRINKING.
SAGE:
BE MORE CARING,
GRACE:
CHANGE YOUR THINKING.
LIZ:
BE ALL I WANT YOU TO BE ...
ALL:
AND YOU'D DO IT ALL GLADLY ... FOR ME.
DENA:
IF YOU REALLY LOVED ME ...
CHLO:
YOU'D STAY WITH ME ON SUNDAYS.
DENA:
IF YOU REALLY LOVED ME ...
SAGE:
YOU'D FORGET FOOTBALL ON MONDAYS.
MOLLY:
YOU'D SAY, "I'LL DO THE MOPPING,"

GRACE:
HELP ME GO CHRISTMAS SHOPPING.
LIZ:
YOU'D SAY, "I'LL SORT THE TAX FILE TODAY!"
ALL:
YOU'D GET YOUR ACT TOGETHER AND DO THINGS MY WAY.
GRACE:
IF YOU REALLY, *REALLY* LOVED ME ...
SAGE:
YOU'D NEVER LOOK AT OTHER LADIES.
GRACE:
IF YOU REALLY, *REALLY* LOVED ME ...
DENA:
YOU'D BUY ME A MERCEDES!
ALL: *(Spoken)* Yes!
SAGE:
YOU'D ALWAYS WALK WHERE I'M WALKING,
CHLO:
NEVER TALK WHEN I'M TALKING,
LIZ:
YOU'D BE JUST THE WAY I'D WANT YOU TO BE ...
ALL:
YOU'D GET YOUR ACT TOGETHER *(GET YOUR ACT TOGETHER)*
AND BE EXACTLY LIKE ... ME!

(At the end of the song, ALL exit except GRACE who re-positions the chairs. OTHERS RE-ENTER. Gradually, DENA's appearance softens.)

LIZ: It just makes my blood boil. She's younger than I am, been with the company fewer years and has the audacity to walk in, close my door and criticize a memo I sent out. Where in the hell does she get off – ? She, she –

CHLO: Sounds like you.

LIZ: Shut the fuck up, Chlo. I don't need your shit today on top of hers.

CHLO: Well, I don't need to hear about this goddam office opponent of yours. You've done her to death.

LIZ: I come here to work off my frustration about office politics so I won't have to at work. That's my prerogative, okay, Chlo? There's no rule that says we can't cover old ground if the ground is still rotten underneath us. Right? Otherwise, we'd stop you everytime you brought up Travis, the son-from-Hell.

CHLO: You watch what you say about him. I'm the only one –

LIZ: Chlo. I love Travis, we all do.

CHLO: And I don't only work on Travis.

LIZ: Bullshit. Ask anyone here. He is your life. He's all consuming. You live –

CHLO: Oh, you have me all figured out, don't you? I –

LIZ: You live in mortal fear of the day he leaves and –

CHLO: Yes. I love my son. Maybe my world does revolve around him. Is that so bad? Is that – ?

LIZ: Because if he ever left, you wouldn't have that crutch –

CHLO: I guess, in your book, it would be wrong.

LIZ: That crutch to avoid your life.

CHLO: To you, children should just be peripheral, disciplined deductions.

LIZ: Now who has whom figured out?

(PAUSE.)

GRACE: Liz, do you want to work on "work"?

LIZ: No.

CHLO: Why don't you just take the other job and leave 'em all in the dust?

LIZ: I still can't bring myself to tell Ron about the job offer.

CHLO: Don't take it.

SAGE: *(To CHLO)* Why not? *(To LIZ)* Why not?

LIZ: Because he's the one who's supposed to get the dream job offer.

MOLLY: I thought you turned them down?

LIZ: That's the problem. I haven't said "no."

CHLO: Bad, bad girl.

LIZ: So, they keep upping their offer.

GRACE: Liz, what's keeping you from discussing this with Ron?

LIZ: He'll blow up. And rightfully so. He's put his career on hold for me.

DENA: What does Ron do?

LIZ: Right now he's a house-husband, but he's studying to be a chef.

GRACE: Are there other things you haven't discussed with Ron?

LIZ: Well, of course, but ... Look, with three teenagers it's like a 24-hour family crisis center at our house. The last thing I would do is open a can of worms between the peacemakers.

CHLO: How is your sex life?

LIZ: Fine and yours?

CHLO: You have the floor, honey.

LIZ: *(Beat)* Ron is very understanding and sensitive ... almost ... too much so.

MOLLY: You have to do what's best for the family.

GRACE: Liz. Tell him. Here.

CHLO: Yeah. I'll be Ron.

LIZ: Wouldn't you love to be?

CHLO: "Love?" No. Adore the challenge? Maybe.

GRACE: Liz, why don't you be Ron and I'll be you?

LIZ: Why don't we just skip it and I'll decline the offer?

GRACE: You're sure?

LIZ: Positive. How is *your* sex life, Chlo, "honey"?

CHLO: Nonexistent, you know that.

LIZ: But the bank had that big party and my stylist friends made you so gorgeous. Did you go alone?

CHLO: No. I went with Madonna.

LIZ: What a shame; an empty seat next to such a pretty lady.

CHLO: Don't give me grief over this now, Liz. I can't "meet" anyone at work things. They're way too conservative. *(Beat)* It's weird. There are a lot of things in me that are shut down. I realized it that night when I went to a bar after. All day at work, I size people up. I look out at them, but never let anyone see into me. No one even approaches.

SAGE: Now you see, me? I always go for those unapproachable types.

MOLLY & LIZ: We know.

CHLO: I'm just at a stage, with a totally straight work environment and a smartass, rapping kid at home.

MOLLY: Travis would be cool about it.

DENA: Yeah. Kids today are pretty worldly.

CHLO: It's not that so much. It's me and my time with him. I don't want to wreck that. Liz, I am going to meet someone as soon as Travis goes away to college. I'll fall tempestuously in love and we'll have a blast and, hopefully, grow old together. But meanwhile I am a single mother trying to raise an adolescent male. That's what I'm here to work on. I'm okay with the other stuff.

LIZ: You are? Well, you may have yourself convinced, but my jury's still out. So sorry to have side-tracked you. By all means, "Travis" away.

(CHLO glares at LIZ.)

DENA: I met Travis. He's not a son-from-Hell.

MOLLY: He's very wise, for someone so young.

SAGE: I'll say. He's more together than I was ... yesterday.

GRACE: *(To DENA)* When did you meet Travis?

DENA: Well, last week after group.

LIZ: Last week? Who invited whom to Chlo's pad? Surely not the shy Ms. Chlo?

GRACE: *(To DENA)* Want to playback a little of that meeting for us? *(DENA shakes her head)* Come on. This will be easy. It will be good for a starter.

DENA: I don't know anyone here well enough to play them.

GRACE: Be Dena. Show us how you met Travis.

(DENA looks at CHLO for a sign. CHLO looks away.)

DENA: Dena is the one person ... I can't be.

GRACE: Then, be Travis and I'll be you.

DENA: I don't think I ... should.

LIZ: This, from an actress?

(GRACE guides DENA and CHLO downstage.)

MOLLY: Come on, be a kid.

SAGE: Yeah, go for it.

DENA: Chlo, do you want me ... ?

CHLO: Yeah, right here, right now! Oh, you're wondering if I want to embarrass myself totally? Sure. Why not? I'll take my medicine. *(Beat. Then to DENA)* What were we talking about when he barged in?

DENA: *(To GRACE, whispered)* Ask her if she and Travis live here alone.

CHLO: No. I live here alone and occasionally Travis drops by.

DENA: *(To GRACE, whispered)* Now tell her she seems so well-adjusted and normal and ask her why –

GRACE: *(As DENA)* Are you in group?

CHLO: I'd go crazy if I wasn't in group. It's funny. You go in crazy and you *stay* in so you don't *go* crazy.

GRACE: *(As DENA)* It can't be as severe as –

CHLO: No. It's maintenance. This is my fourth group and each time I find new things to work on.

GRACE: *(As DENA)* Good.

CHLO: I think of group as a utility. Each month you need gas, electricity, phone and group! *(Beat)* And that's when Travis came in.

DENA: I can't.

SAGE: Sure you can.

LIZ: Did he rap? Travis always raps.

DENA: Yes. But I couldn't possibly attempt ...

GRACE: Just come as close as you can.

SONG: "YO, CHLO" *(DENA [As TRAVIS])*

LIZ:
WAS IT A SMOOTH GROOVE?

DENA: *(Spoken)* Yes, but I can't ...

LIZ:
WAS IT A SNAP RAP?

DENA: *(Spoken)* Well, I guess.
LIZ:
PUT ON A CAP RAP?

(She hands her a baseball cap.)

DENA: *(Spoken)* Oh. This is painful.
CHLO:
(Bravely)
CUT THE CRAP, RAP!

(MUSIC BEGINS. DENA walks around and gets into TRAVIS'
character.)

DENA: *(as TRAVIS)*
YO, CHLO. WHOA! WHADDA WE GOT?
THE MOM'S WITH A FRIEND, AND THE FRIEND IS HOT.
OOOO, SHE SIZZLES, I DEHYDRATE,
KNOCK ME OVER WITH A FEATHER, COULD THIS BE A
    DATE?
CHLO: *(Spoken)* You're totally off-base.
DENA: *(As TRAVIS)*
THAT'S NOT WHAT I SEE IN YOUR FACE.
GO, CHLO. I LIKE YA LIKE THIS.
SO, CHLO. LOVE STRIKE YA LIKE THIS?
WHOA, LOOK AT THE BLOOD RUSH TO MOM'S HEAD,
YO, LOOK AT HER SKIN TURN KETCHUP RED.
WORD: FOX. AHOOOOOOOOO!
CHLO: *(Spoken)* Dena. this is my son, Travis. Travis, this is
Dena White.
DENA: *(As TRAVIS)*
DENA WHITE, DENA WHITE
THAT NAME RINGS A BELL.
THE FILE FINDER SAYS,
I KNOW IT WELL.
DENA WHITE! DENA WHITE!
GOT YOUR RECORDS, I'LL SHOW YA.
YOU'RE A SILVER-THROAT SONGBIRD

I'M REAL GLAD TO KNOW YA.

WORD: CLASSY.

> **CHLO:** *(Spoken)* She came over to look at your records. To see what a "normal" fourteen-year-old's musical tastes are like.

> **DENA:** *(As TRAVIS)*

SCOPE! HOPE THE LADY LIKES THE HOUSEHOLD WEATHER.

IF SHE LIKES THE KID'S DISCS, DO WE ALL LIVE TOGETHER?

> **CHLO:** *(Spoken)* Travis, would you stop insinuating?

> **DENA:** *(As TRAVIS)*

YO, CHLO, NO USE UNLOOSING,

I'M GATHERING THE FACTS, I AM DEFTLY DEDUCING.

HOW MANY TIMES YOU BROUGHT A LADY HOME?

TAKE A GUESS, CHLO. HAS IT BEEN A TON?

TAKE A GUESS, CHLO. HAVE YOU BROUGHT HOME ONE?

WORD: NONE.

> **CHLO:** *(Spoken)* He usually doesn't rap this long. He must want something.

> **GRACE:** *(As DENA. Spoken)* I should be going anyway.

> **CHLO:** *(Spoken)* Now see what you've done?

> **DENA:** *(As TRAVIS)*

HOLD THE PHONE, CHLONE, YOUR TONE'S LIKE A GORE,

THE CHANTEUSE IS STRAIGHT; YOU WEREN'T GONNA SCORE.

> **CHLO:** *(Spoken)* Scoring isn't the point! Dena is a friend, someone I admire and you've embarrassed me!

> **DENA:** *(As TRAVIS)*

RELEASE THE NEWS! WHITE HOUSE ALERT!

DUMB SON EMBARE-ASSES MOM AND GETS HURT.

THAT'S A CRIME, BOY. YOU'LL PAY PLENTY,

A JURY WILL CONVICT YOU, AND YOU'LL DO TWENTY.

THE BOY NEEDS A PUSH, THE BOY NEEDS A SHOVE,

THE BOY IS A NERD ONLY A MOTHER COULD LOVE.

WORD: GEEK.

> **CHLO:** *(Spoken)* Let's talk about this later.

DENA: *(As TRAVIS)*
THERE'S ALWAYS A LATER, THERE'S ALWAYS A WAIT,
THEN LATER GETS LATER AND LATER'S TOO LATE.
LET'S NOT PUT IT OFF, LET'S NOT WAIT A DAY,
LET'S TALK IT OUT NOW, RIGHT FUCKING AWAY.

ON SECOND THOUGHT, I'M GOING TO MY ROOM,
I'M SHUTTING THE DOOR TO ESCAPE MY DOOM.
WHEN YOU KNOCK LATER ON, I WON'T LET YOU IN,
ANOTHER NIGHT LOST, NO ONE GETS TO WIN.
'CAUSE YOU DON'T UNDERSTAND
OF MY SOUL, I'M THE OWNER.
MAN! I WISH I KNEW THE NAME
OF THAT SPERM DONOR.

(She stops. The others applaud. DENA tosses the cap to LIZ.)

SAGE: Dena, you were a sensationally, assholey Travis. I am just totally blown away.
CHLO: Yeah. Wow. *(To DENA)* What a great Travis. Maybe you could come home and say all the things I want Travis to say.
DENA: Chlo, you've got a great kid.

(MUSIC BEGINS.)

CHLO: *(Beat)* I love him so much. I can't get through. He's shut me out. If he'd just run to me like he used to. Laugh. Hug me once in a while.

SONG: "IF YOU REALLY LOVED ME" (Reprise) *(CHLO)*

CHLO:
IF YOU REALLY LOVED ME
YOU'D BE TINY AGAIN.
IF YOU REALLY LOVED ME
YOU'D BE LIKE YOU WERE THEN.
YOU WOULD ANXIOUSLY PLEASE ME
DO WHAT I TOLD YOU

REACH OUT AND NEED ME
JUST LET ME HOLD YOU
BE SOFT, BE SWEET
SIT ON MY LAP
AND DANCE ON MY FEET.

IF YOU REALLY LOVED ME
YOU'D HAVE NEVER GROWN UP.
IF YOU REALLY LOVED ME
YOU'D HAVE NEVER GROWN TOUGH.
YOU'D BE PERFECTLY CHARMING
POLITE AND DISARMING
A PICTURE OF WISDOM AND CALM
YOU'D GET YOUR ACT TOGETHER
AND BE A PRINCE LIKE YOUR MOM.

SONG: Scene Change 2

(CHLO takes off her blazer and rolls up her sleeves and sits down. The OTHERS enter and take different seats.)

CHLO: Dena, I don't understand. You've got a beautiful voice.

DENA: But that's not what radio wants.

MOLLY: What do they want?

DENA: Teenagers.

SAGE: But you don't sound old ... do you?

CHLO: But last night you sounded great.

LIZ: Where? What'd I miss?

CHLO: Harry managed to convince Dena to sing.

MOLLY: And then you ran out? Why?

GRACE: What happened?

MOLLY: It was just a dinner party.

GRACE: You want to show us?

DENA: No!

CHLO: Boy, no one knows more about Dena than Harry. Talk about a fan.

GRACE: Show us the evening.

DENA: No. I can't. It was ...

GRACE: Harry convinced you to sing?

DENA: Yeah.

GRACE: Then you be Harry. I want to see you be someone who admires you. Okay?

DENA: Grace, no. I ...

GRACE: And Molly, you be Dena and Chlo, you be Molly.

MOLLY: Who will be Chlo?

SAGE: I will.

CHLO: But you weren't there.

SAGE: You said you were a bump on a log. I can handle that.

DENA: I don't really think I ... I can't.

GRACE: If it gets too difficult, we'll stop.

(DENA, CHLO, MOLLY and SAGE cross to another area. LIZ and GRACE watch. MOLLY wears DENA's sunglasses. CHLO makes the sound of a knock.)

CHLO: *(As MOLLY)* Right on time. *(She opens an imaginary door)* Come on in.

MOLLY: *(As DENA)* Oh. This place is enchanting.

CHLO: *(As MOLLY)* Thanks. We call it mini-Tara. *(DENA enters as HARRY)* Oh, Dena. This speechless person is my husband, Harry.

SAGE: *(As CHLO)* Harry, ol' boy. How're they hangin'?

CHLO: *I* would never say that.

SAGE: Sorry.

CHLO: Think of something else.

SAGE: *(As CHLO)* How about them Mets?

MOLLY: *(As DENA)* Hi, Harry.

DENA: *(As HARRY)* Hi. I expected you to look older.

MOLLY: *(As DENA)* Molly, I love him. Can I have him when you're done?

DENA: *(As HARRY)* You can have me now.

CHLO: *(As MOLLY)* I chilled some champagne. Dena, please join us.

MOLLY: *(As DENA)* Twist my arm. Okay, okay. I give in. Where are the kids?

CHLO: *(As MOLLY)* With their Grandma.

MOLLY: *(As DENA)* I wanted to meet them.

CHLO: *(As MOLLY)* We'll show you a video and that way you can turn them off or down.

(SAGE [As CHLO] laughs a very hearty laugh. CHLO glares at her.)

CHLO: "Bump!" "On a log!" Remember?

(HARRY pops the champagne cork and pours three glasses.)

DENA: *(As HARRY)* Here's to your next record.

CHLO: *(As MOLLY)* May it be soon.

MOLLY: *(As DENA)* Thanks and here's to your darling children.

DENA: *(As HARRY. Looking at MOLLY [As DENA])* Here's to beautiful women.

(They ALL drink, except MOLLY.)

MOLLY: Did he say that?

DENA: Yes.

MOLLY: I didn't hear it. He said that and looked at you?

DENA: Uh ... yes.

CHLO: And then we all proceeded to get quietly drunk.

GRACE: Care to go on?

MOLLY: *(As DENA)* I can't believe you bought all my albums.

DENA: *(As HARRY)* You know, I'd kill to have you do "Until Tonight."

MOLLY: *(As DENA)* No. Really, no. I ... haven't sung in anyone's living room in oodles of ... long time.

DENA: *(As HARRY)* We'll turn out the lights. Okay? We have a spotlight over the piano. *(DENA [As HARRY] stands in front of MOLLY [As DENA] and holds her by the shoulders quite suggestively)* Please? I'll love it. I promise.

MOLLY: Hold it. Dena, aren't you overdoing this flirting thing with Harry a little?

DENA: No. If anything I'm downplaying it. You ought to know, you were there.

MOLLY: I didn't see anything that ... Did Harry ... ?

DENA: Yes.

MOLLY: How could he be so obvious with me there?

CHLO: He always is. He's a flirt.

LIZ: Lots of men flirt, Molly.

MOLLY: Stop.

DENA: I'm sorry if I –

MOLLY: Don't. I ... Maybe it was just because he's in awe of you.

DENA: I hardly think –

CHLO: Molly, hon. Face it –

MOLLY: Chlo, shut up! The wound is wide open. No salt please.

GRACE: *(Beat)* Molly, are you all right? *(MOLLY nods)* Do you want to work on this now?

(MOLLY shakes her head. GRACE looks to the others to see if anyone else is ready to work.)

LIZ: *(Beat)* Dena. You've been absent from the scene for so long now. You have to let people know you're still here *and* vibrant *and* viable! Do a live show.

DENA: Oh, sure. I'll just whip one up. Do an evening of my one hit, nine different ways.

CHLO: Instead of wimping about it, why not show them?

DENA: Because I cannot get up, stand there and muster the confidence ... to make believe that I'm a singer again ... a person anymore.

LIZ: Dena, what I was driving at is that this won't work unless you're totally honest in here.

GRACE: Dena, have you been honest?

DENA: Yes.

LIZ: I checked and you don't have a recording contract.

MOLLY: That's ridiculous.

LIZ: Maybe, but true. You filed for a Chapter Eleven and I checked with the musicians' union and you haven't worked in four years; not even backup.

CHLO: Why?

DENA: *(To LIZ, stunned)* You did that?

LIZ: Well, my secretary ...

CHLO: What have you been doing for four years, Dena?

DENA: I've been concentrating on my ... writing.

LIZ: You're broke, aren't you?

SAGE: But if you had a Number One Hit, don't you have, like, trillions of dollars?

DENA: No. The chart is based on radio play and sales, so –

GRACE: Dena, why don't we discuss this afterward? Perhaps we can –

DENA: *(To LIZ)* Put that away. I don't want your charity.

LIZ: I insist. I'm writing you a season pass.

DENA: No! I don't want to owe you anything.

GRACE: Liz, I'll handle this after –

LIZ: No strings attached.

DENA: How can you even begin to – ? You've got more money than you know what to do with.

LIZ: That's not true. I work extremely hard and still have to watch every –

DENA: Hard labor, I'm sure. You have no idea what it's like to scrimp and –

LIZ: I took loans to go to college, waitressed through graduate school, filed during three pregnancies –

DENA: You weren't alone!

LIZ: It's not like it was handed to me.

DENA: I've worked too. Just as hard. But for what I do, they don't give you a check at the end of every week just for coming to work.

GRACE: Dena, we have a thing we do sometimes, called "Behind My Back." It's usually requested by a member and she invites the others to talk behind her back – only she's there.

LIZ: It's good.

MOLLY: It's hell, but it's good.

GRACE: Do you want us to show you?

DENA: Are you trying to suggest *I* request it?

GRACE: It takes a lot of courage and if you don't feel you can –

DENA: Grace. Is this what you call giving it my best shot?

MOLLY: No. This is called taking shots.

SAGE: Go on. It'll be good for you.

CHLO: We'll aim low.

(MUSIC BEGINS.)

SONG: "BEHIND DENA's BACK" *(ALL)*

SAGE:

I'VE DONE HER NUMBERS MANY TIMES
AND NO MATTER WHAT I TRY
SHE COMES UP FAMOUS AND HAPPY.
I KNOW SHE'S GOT IT IN HER STARS
TO BE EVERYTHING SHE WANTS
INCLUDING FAMOUS AND HAPPY.
IF SHE COULD SEE HERSELF THE WAY I SEE HER,
SHE'D BE ABSOLUTELY THRILLED TO BE HER.

LIZ:

I DON'T KNOW WHY SHE'S SO UPSET.
SHE'S HAD MORE THAN MOST PEOPLE GET.
SHE DIDN'T DO HALF BAD.
SHE SHOULD BE MORE THAN GLAD.
SHE HAD HER MOMENT IN THE SUN.
THAT DOESN'T HAPPEN TO EVERYONE.

CHLO:

SHE IS SO BEAUTIFUL.
AND SHE DOESN'T KNOW IT.
SHE'S AFRAID OF GETTING OLDER,
BUT HER BODY DOESN'T SHOW IT.
SHE'S A FLOWER JUST STARTING TO GROW.
I LOVE HER, BUT I COULD NEVER TELL HER SO.

MOLLY:

IT'S A FANTASY FOR SURE,
BUT I SEE ME IN HER.
SHE NEEDS A BABY IN HER LIFE.

I THINK THERE'S PART OF HER
THAT WANTS TO BE A WIFE.
AND THAT PART OF ME IN HER,
THAT PART OF HER ALLURE
THAT HARRY CAN PLAINLY SEE
IS WHY HE'LL STAY WITH ME.
    DENA:
I'M SO SORRY I HURT YOU.
    MOLLY:
YOU'RE NOT SUPPOSED TO TALK.
WE'RE TALKING BEHIND YOUR BACK.
    DENA:
THERE'S NO WAY
I'D EVER WANT TO HURT YOU.
    LIZ:
YOU HAD IT ALL, DENA
I'D KILL TO HAVE YOUR TALENT.
YOU HAD FAME AND FORTUNE,
AND THE LOVE OF A MAN.
YOU LOST IT ALL, DENA
YOU DIDN'T HAVE A PLAN.
    CHLO:
SHUT UP, LIZ
YOU DON'T KNOW WHAT SHE NEEDS.
    DENA:
I NEED SUPPORT, GRACE.
NOT SOMEONE SELLING ME SHORT, GRACE.
    GRACE:
NO ONE CAN SELL YOU SHORT
BUT YOU.
SOMETIMES THE BEST SUPPORT
IF BEING PUSHED
AND GETTING SHOVED.
SPEAK YOUR HEART, DENA.
LET THE REAL YOU BE LOVED.

SONG: "NO ONE INSIDE" *(DENA)*

   DENA:
WHEN I LOOK IN THE MIRROR
I SEE NO ONE THERE.
THERE'S A FRAME OF A BODY,
THERE'S A FACE AND HAIR.
BUT THE PERSON I AM
ISN'T ANYWHERE.
THERE'S NO ONE INSIDE.
NO ONE INSIDE.

WHAT YOU'RE SAYING IS WRONG,
'CAUSE YOU DON'T KNOW ME,
I'M AN IMAGE OF SOMEONE
WHO'S A FANTASY.
THERE'S A HOLLOW RIGHT HERE
WHERE A SOUL SHOULD BE.
WHERE IS THE PRIDE?
NO ONE INSIDE.

I DON'T KNOW WHAT TO DO.
I DON'T KNOW WHAT TO SAY.
WHO SHOULD I BE TODAY?

I CAN GO IT ALONE
I AM PLENTY STRONG
I DON'T NEED YOUR SUPPORT,
I DON'T WANT TO BELONG.
DON'T NEED ANYONE TELLING ME
RIGHT FROM WRONG.
PERSON DENIED.
NO ONE INSIDE.

I SAY THAT I UNDERSTAND
PRETEND THAT I'M DOING FINE
BUT I CAN'T EVEN LEND A HAND
TO SOMEONE WHOSE PAIN IS GREATER THAN MINE.

WHEN I OPEN MY EYES
AND I LOOK AROUND,
ALL I SEE ARE REMAINS
OF THE DREAM THAT DROWNED,
AND I CAN'T SEEM TO REACH
FOR A HIGHER GROUND ...
NOBODY THERE,
NO ONE, NOWHERE.

I DON'T KNOW WHAT TO DO.
I DON'T KNOW WHAT TO SAY.
THERE'S NOTHING LEFT FOR ME TO BE TODAY.

SAGE: There, now. Don't you feel better?

DENA: No. I feel ... I think I'm going to leave.

SAGE: Please stay. You can't go out there like that. Your mind's all opened up. Someone will jump in and then you'll really be violated beyond natural repair.

MOLLY: Stay, Dena.

SAGE: You're improved, Dena. Take my word for it.

DENA: How can you know?

SAGE: Because I did your chart and by now you were scheduled to be really fucked up. But you're not. See?

LIZ: Dena, maybe you *should* leave because you're wasting our time.

MOLLY: Now, Liz, I'm sorry. But I have to say something. We've got to draw the line somewhere! You're so concerned with the value of time and getting your fair share that you've lost all sensitivity. What a horrid thing to say to Dena!! Ooh. Did I just get aggressive?

LIZ: If you'd let me finish, you'd see my point.

MOLLY: Well can't you get there a little less rudely?!

LIZ: What I said was for effect and you've ruined it.

MOLLY: *(To LIZ)* Sorry. *(To DENA)* Sorry. *(To HERSELF)* I'm apologizing for getting aggressive. No one else does that.

DENA: *(To LIZ)* Who in the hell do you think you are? Success? You're the one who's deluded. You think you're getting better every time you come here? It's a drug. You get to come in and bitch and people actually listen. I can't afford *your* habit.

LIZ: *(To ALL)* Forget it.
DENA: No. You forget it!

(MUSIC BEGINS. LIGHTS FADE on group area and Individual Pools of Light FADE UP. ALL take places in separate lights.)

SONG: "INSIDE OUT" (Reprise)

DENA:
WHY DID I SAY THAT?
LIZ:
WHAT WAS I THINKING?
SAGE & MOLLY:
WHERE DO I START?

LIZ & CHLO:	**DENA, MOLLY, SAGE:**
WHY DID I SAY THAT?	WHY DID I SAY THAT?
WHAT WAS I THINKING?	WHAT WAS I THINKING?
WHERE DO I START?	WHERE DO I START?

3-PART VOICES IN A ROUND:
WHY DID I SAY THAT?
WHAT WAS I THINKING?
WHERE DO I START?

WHY DID I SAY THAT?
WHAT WAS I THINKING?
WHERE DO I START?

ALL: *(Except GRACE)*
CAN I CLIMB OVER THE WALL
AROUND MY HEART?

GRACE:	**LIZ:**
FIND A WAY IN,	CAN I DECIDE?
OPEN A DOOR,	CAN I SPEAK MY MIND?
	MOLLY:
WALK THROUGH YOUR	WHERE IS THE WOMAN
MIRROR OF DOUBT,	I HAVE NEVER BEEN?

GO PAST THE SKIN,

CHLO:
CAN I BE LOVED?
DENA:
RIGHT TO THE CORE,   JUST BE MYSELF.
AREN'T YOU ALL LIED OUT?
    ALL: **ALL:**
ALL CRIED OUT.   ALL CRIED OUT?
   VOICES 1, 2, 3   **VOICES 4, 5, 6**
ROLL UP THE SHADES   HOW AM I GONNA
                      SURVIVE?
NO MORE CHARADES   HOW CAN I FEEL
                    MORE ALIVE?
    ALL:
I MAKE A VOW,
STARTING RIGHT NOW
TO TAKE A NEW ROUTE,
AND TURN THE INSIDE OUT.

(CURTAIN ACT ONE.)

ACT TWO

SONG: "GRACE'S NIGHTMARE" *(GRACE & COMPANY)*

GRACE:
HELLO, DR. JORDAN?
THIS IS GRACE, LONG DISTANCE.
I KNOW THIS MAY SOUND CRAZY
BUT I NEED YOUR ASSISTANCE.
I HAVE A GROUP THAT MEETS ONCE A WEEK
BUT I SEE THEM MORE OFTEN THAN THAT.
THEY SEEM TO BE HERE WHEN THEY'RE NOT HERE,
AND I DON'T KNOW EXACTLY HOW THEY GOT HERE.
LIZ:
I DON'T MEAN TO INTERRUPT YOU.
MOLLY:
BUT I'VE GOT TO TALK TO SOMEONE.
SAGE & CHLO:
YOU'RE THE ONLY ONE
WHO KNOWS WHAT I SHOULD DO.

GRACE:	**OTHERS:**
(Spoken) More shit!	
(Sung)	
HOW TO EXPLAIN?	HA HA
IT'S VERY HARD.	HA HA
THEY ARE IN THE	
KITCHEN CUPBOARD,	HA HA
THEY ARE IN THE YARD.	HA HA
IN EVERY PLATE	HA HA
OR POT OF TEA,	HA HA
I SEE ONE OF THEIR FACES	
STARING BACK AT ME.	

MOLLY:
YOO-HOO, GRACE!
DO YOU THINK MY FACE IS FAT?

CHLO:
WHAT DO YOU THINK, GRACE?
MOLLY:
CAN I SHRINK, GRACE?
SAGE:
IF YOU REALLY LOVED ME...
CHLO:
REALLY LOVED ME
LIZ:
WHAT DO YOU THINK, GRACE?
SAGE:
YOU WOULD TELL ME WHAT TO DO.

GRACE:	**OTHERS:**
WHY HAVE A GROUP?	HUH!
WHERE DOES IT LEAD?	HUH!
THE MORE I GIVE,	HUH!
THE MORE THEY NEED.	HUH!
I HEAR THEIR VOICES	HUH!
IN THE AIR.	HUH!

DENA:
CAN I EVER BE A STAR?
SAGE:
CAN YOU FLY ME TO THE MOON?
MOLLY:
IS MY LIFE A CANDY BAR?

DENA:
WILL I HAVE A HIT SOON?
LIZ:
TIME TO GO TO WORK, TIME TO MAKE A CALL,
GRACE:
DR. JORDAN, ARE YOU THERE?
LIZ:
WILL HE STAY, GRACE?
CAN I HAVE A PERK? CAN I HAVE IT ALL?
GRACE:
THIS IS MORE THAN I CAN BEAR.
LIZ:
WHAT DO YOU SAY, GRACE?

GRACE:
THEY'VE ALL GOT PROBLEMS TO WORK THROUGH,
I DON'T KNOW WHAT THEY'RE GOING TO DO,
SOMETIMES I WISH I COULD
FIX THEM ON THE SPOT.
I KNOW IT ISN'T UP TO ME,
IT'S THEIR RESPONSIBILITY,
STILL I WANT THEM TO SEE
WHAT THEY ARE NOT *(NOT, NOT)*
AND WHAT THEY ARE *(ARE, ARE)*
AND HOW A LITTLE WORK CAN TAKE THEM VERY FAR.
(VERY FAR)
MOLLY:
MY CAKE IS SAUTÉED.
THE LETTUCE IS BROWN,
THE EGGS I JUST LAID
ARE SUNNY SIDE DOWN.
GRACE, WHAT DO I DO?
ALL:
WHAT DO I DO, GRACE?
GRACE:
I'VE RUN A GROUP
THREE TIMES OR FOUR,
BUT I SWEAR
THIS NEVER HAPPENED BEFORE.
THEY FILL MY DREAMS,
DESTROY MY SLEEP.
DO YOU THINK
I'VE GOTTEN IN TOO DEEP?
MOLLY:
FAT,
I WANNA BE FAT,
I WANNA BE FAT.
SAGE:
EVERY TIME THE CARDS SAY, "HI!"
MY HEART SAYS, "DIE!"
MOLLY, DENA & LIZ:
WHY JOIN A GROUP?

SAGE:
EVERY TIME THE STARS SAY, "SCHMUCK."
MY HEART SAYS, *(Pause, then quickly)* "DUCK!"
   MOLLY, DENA & LIZ:
WHY JOIN A GROUP?
   SAGE:
HOW CAN I TELL THE TRUTH I KNOW,
I WAS A GYPSY LONG AGO.
   CHLO:
CLOTHES ARE NOT MY THING,
PAINTING IS MY THING,
I'D LIKE TO DRAW MY CLOTHES TODAY,
WALK IN IN THE RAW TODAY.
WHAT DO YOU SAY, GRACE, WHAT DO YOU SAY?
   GRACE:
YES, I'VE BEEN WORKING DAY AND NIGHT,
NO, MY MARRIAGE IS ALL RIGHT,
YES, I'M DOING AN APPEARANCE ON TV.
   (YEAH, YEAH, YEAH.)
AM I AFRAID I WON'T BE GOOD?
SCARED I'LL BE MISUNDERSTOOD?
DOCTOR, YOU DON'T HAVE TO
PULL THAT CRAP ON ME!
THIS IS GRACE – A MAJOR HAM!
WELL, MAYBE JUST A LITTLE, YES I AM.

GRACE:	**OTHERS:**
IS IT THE GROUP?	IS IT THE GROUP?
OR IS IT ME?	OR IS IT ME?
HAVE I FINALLY REACHED	
THE LIMIT OF MY SANITY?	
IT'S MENOPAUSE!	*(Spoken)* Nope!
THAT'S WHAT IT IS!	*(Spoken)* Uh-oh!
MID-LIFE CRISIS	
WASN'T BAD ENOUGH,	
NOW THIS!	NOW THIS, NOW THIS!
THANK YOU SO MUCH,	THANK YOU SO MUCH,
OH YES, I'M SURE.	OH YES, I'M SURE

YOU THINK A WEEK
   IN THE BAHAMAS
IS THE PERFECT CURE.   *(Spoken)* What?
A LOT OF SEX   *(Spoken)* Oh?
A LITTLE REST.   *(Spoken)* Ah.
OH, DOCTOR,
YOUR PRESCRIPTIONS
ARE THE BEST!   THE BEST, THE BEST!

     MOLLY, SAGE, LIZ, CHLO & DENA:
GRACE, I NEED TO TALK,
I NEED TO HEAR,
I NEED TO SEE,
I THINK I FEEL
REJECTED, UNLOVED, STUPID, FAT, CONFUSED,
   UNWORTHY.

     LIZ, CHLO, SAGE:
AM I DOING WHAT I SHOULD?

     MOLLY:
I'M FAT. I'M FAT. I'M FAT. I'M FAT ...

     DENA:
I WANT A HIT, GRACE, A HIT.

     GRACE:
I don't know!! That's your problem!!! *(Beat)* God, that felt good!

(BLACKOUT)

SONG: Scene Change 3

(LIGHTS COME UP on Group in session.)

    GRACE: *(To CHLO)* Why do you worry?

    CHLO: I'm a mother. My mother worried about me. I worry about him.

    DENA: What would happen if you didn't worry?

    CHLO: He'd get into trouble.

    GRACE: You're telling us that as long as you worry, he won't get into trouble?

MOLLY: Do you trust Travis?

CHLO: Yes.

GRACE: So, why don't you let him pick his own curfew?

CHLO: He'll pick four in the morning!

GRACE: Within reason.

LIZ: Any kid who wants trouble, doesn't have to abuse a curfew to get into it.

CHLO: Okay. I'll give it a try.

GRACE: Good.

SAGE: You should think warm, safe thoughts about Travis if he's out late. Put "white light" around him. That's what I do when Garth has to fly.

CHLO: Well, at least he's honest.

DENA: How do you know?

CHLO: Mothers just do. Right, Mothers?

LIZ: I can spot a lie a mile away.

GRACE: Me, too.

MOLLY: What's so funny is how smug they get when they think they've conned you.

GRACE: Who still lies to their mother?

LIZ: Not me.

MOLLY: Oh, mine can see right through me.

SAGE: My mother never believed me even when I was telling the truth.

GRACE: Dena, do you?

DENA: No, I ...

CHLO: What do you lie about?

DENA: I just said I ...

LIZ: And I think all the mothers here saw through that one.

(DENA stands up and moves away from the group and looks out an imaginary window.)

SAGE: We won't tell. Everything we share here is totally top-secret.

DENA: I don't lie to her, I just haven't ... well, corrected what she thinks.

LIZ: Which is ... ?

DENA: She has boxes of records and tapes in her garage. And whenever she meets someone new she gives them one. She has pictures, programs, scrapbooks ...

CHLO: She thinks everything is still going strong?

LIZ: But you haven't had a record out in four years.

DENA: I've told her that the next one is real important; that it has to be just right and that's why it's taking five years.

GRACE: How often do you see her?

DENA: I don't! I haven't in – four or five months. She calls and I let the machine pick up. I pretend to be away, busy. That's what she wants, so I let her have it.

MOLLY: I'm sure she'd understand.

DENA: But why give her the grief?

SAGE: God, if I couldn't unload on my mom, I'd have to do two or three group therapies.

GRACE: Dena, why are you hiding behind screened calls?

DENA: It's just easier than explaining or pretending.

SAGE: What do you do all day?

CHLO: She writes songs.

LIZ: When you're not writing?

DENA: I don't write! Okay? *(Beat)* I watch ... the bus stop below my window. I know everybody who takes that bus and when they go to work. I know all their clothes and when they get something new. They all have lives.

MOLLY: You do, too.

DENA: No. I did. Sometimes I don't feel worthy to step outside, to stand at the bus stop because that bus shouldn't stop for me.

SAGE: I've had buses go right by me even if I pound on the door.

DENA: I stayed in for almost ten whole days, once.

GRACE: Dena, I think there are times we all want to hide, to be ostriches. Don't hate yourself for that. You did what you needed to; you're taking steps.

SAGE: But you're not done yet.

LIZ: And you can't keep hiding.

SAGE: You've got to do that cabaret.

MOLLY: Yes!

GRACE: Make it a goal, a purpose.

DENA: It's so overwhelming. I ...

LIZ: We'll help.

MOLLY: Yeah. We'll make it a group group effort.

SAGE: Hey. I just thought of something. I know this guy who comes into the store all the time. He has a club that used to be a coffeehouse. I'll bet I could get him to get us a deal.

MOLLY: Harry would help, too. He knows lots of people.

CHLO: I could do a backdrop.

SAGE: I'll make flyers and give them to customers.

LIZ: Ron and I could cater it. He makes this great – Oh, listen to us. We sound like a regular, Mickey & Judy: "Let's put on a show!"

SAGE: I would not offer a barn. This is a nice club.

DENA: No, you guys. I'm just not ready. There are a lot of things I need to straighten out before I can ... That's why I'm here.

LIZ: Okay. Let's make a list. You have to start somewhere.

DENA: I'm sick of feeling sorry for myself and I keep hoping someone will come and magically revive everything. *(Beat)* I am broke. Really. And putting a cabaret act together isn't a cheap thing.

GRACE: You've just had lots of offers to help.

DENA: I know. That's great. Really. It's the first positive thing ... But I'd need charts, rehearsal time, clothes ... I'm all tapped out. And I've looked for job-jobs to help me pay for those things, but no one's taking.

MOLLY: Chlo, what about something at Citibank?

CHLO: I don't know. I was actually just thinking about it and –

SAGE: Liz, how about a job at your cosmetic company?

DENA: No, you guys don't understand.

(MUSIC BEGINS.)

SONG: "ALL I DO IS SING" *(DENA)*

DENA:
I DON'T KNOW WHAT TO DO.

ALL I DO IS SING.

    GRACE: *(Spoken)* Then sing.

    DENA:

I NEED A SHOW, IT'S TRUE ...

GOTTA GRAB THAT BRASS RING.

UNDERSTAND, I REALLY CANNOT TYPE.

    CHLO: *(Spoken)* Don't type.

    DENA:

UNDERSTAND, I REALLY CANNOT SELL.

    LIZ: *(Spoken)* Don't sell.

    DENA:

THERE IS NOTHING ELSE I DO VERY WELL.

    LIZ: *(Spoken)* You don't have to.

    DENA:

CAN YOU SEE ME SHOWING PERFUME

IN A LARGE DEPARTMENT STORE

SAYING, "JUST A DAB WILL MAKE YOU

MORE ATTRACTIVE THAN BEFORE?"

CAN YOU SEE ME CHECKING GROCERIES

ASKING, "PAPER OR PLASTIC?"

PUNCHING NUMBERS IN COMPUTERS

TRYING TO BE ENTHUSIASTIC?

TIL SOMEBODY SAYS, "HEY, AREN'T YOU..?"

AND I MUMBLE, "YES."

SOMEONE ELSE SAYS, "DENA WHITE, AREN'T YOU?"

AND I CRUMBLE, "YES."

DENA WHITE, THAT BRILLIANT SUCCESS.

WELL, I'VE BEEN A GROC'RY CHECKER

AND I'VE SOLD PERFUME.

I'VE MADE FLORAL ARRANGEMENTS

IN SOMEBODY'S BACK ROOM.

I HAVE ANSWERED SOMEONE'S PHONES

SAYING, "JUST A MOMENT, PLEASE."

I HAVE DEMONSTRATED BLENDERS

SMILING WHILE I GRATED CHEESE.

BUT I CAN'T DO THAT ANYMORE.
I'VE GOT TOO MUCH AT STAKE.
IF I DON'T GET OUT
AND PERFORM I'LL BREAK.

I WAS BORN TO SING.
I CAN'T DO ANYTHING
BUT POUR MY GUTS OUT IN A SONG.
I MUST MOVE AHEAD
CAUSE THAT'S WHAT I NEED,
AND WISHING WON'T MAKE IT SO,
CAN I MAKE THAT DOOR
OPEN ONCE MORE?
OR IS THAT GOAL TOO HIGH?
I'LL NEVER,
I'LL NEVER
I'LL NEVER KNOW 'TIL I TRY.

(They ALL rush to DENA, and embrace her.)

SONG: Scene Change 4

(LIGHT PATTERNS CHANGE. They reposition their chairs. SAGE exits. They ALL sit, except SAGE.)

    LIZ: *(To DENA)* How did your jingle session go?

    DENA: It was so simple and they loved me. Thank you, Liz, so much.

    MOLLY: So you're going to be singing for commercials?

    LIZ: Momentarily. Hey, where's Sage?

    GRACE: I don't know. It's not like her to be late.

    DENA: *(To GRACE)* Was that your husband I saw you with in the lobby?

    GRACE: That was my ex.

    LIZ: Which ex?

    GRACE: The second.

    DENA: You mean you're on your third marriage?

    LIZ: Yeah. Can you believe that? And she has the nerve to tell us how to fix our marriages.

GRACE: No. I've never told anyone how to "fix" anything. And I've never made a pretense that I was the perfect spouse. I do know what can go wrong.

DENA: Could you introduce me to #2 and tell me what not to do with him?

GRACE: Well, he's involved.

DENA: Yeah. It's no wonder. He's beautiful.

MOLLY: And aren't they getting progressively younger, Grace?

GRACE: Well, yes.

MOLLY: You keep them all such secrets.

CHLO: Not true. She just doesn't take up our time talking about her home life because Liz would demand a credit memo.

LIZ: I would not.

GRACE: It isn't really appropriate for me to discuss my private life here. And my third marriage isn't perfect, but –

(SAGE runs in very over-dressed and heavily made-up.)

SAGE: Sorry, I'm late.
CHLO: Get a load of you.
MOLLY: Sage, you look so ... different.
SAGE: Do you like it?

(ALL are speechless.)

MOLLY: Why did you do it?

SAGE: Well, last week I tried it and Garth hated it, so I did it again.

DENA: Why doesn't Garth like you like this?

LIZ: Did he think you were saving mascara for your wedding?

MOLLY: Wedding? What? Did I miss something? Did Garth propose?

SAGE: No, but ...
MOLLY: But what?
SAGE: I did.

DENA: What did he say?

SAGE: He said that if I needed rings and legal documents to trap and bind him, he'd concede.

LIZ: A true romantic.

GRACE: Are you seeing Garth tonight?

SAGE: Yeah. We're going to a tofu-tasting party.

MOLLY: Go like that.

DENA: Do it.

LIZ: I'd love to know what his reaction is.

CHLO: I know what he'd say.

SAGE: No, you don't.

CHLO: Oh, yes, I do. Remember that eternity I spent with Garth waiting for you at the bloodmobile?

GRACE: Let's try something. We'll say, you're at that party tonight; now. And Chlo, you're Garth.

(SAGE and CHLO cross to another area.)

SAGE: Don't my eyes look hazeler? (*or: periwinkler)*

CHLO: *(as GARTH)* Yes.

SAGE: You said you loved my hazel eyes. *(or: periwinkle)* Don't you love them more hazely? *(or: periwinkly)*

CHLO: *(as GARTH)* No. I liked it better when they were a well-kept secret.

SAGE: So, you're jealous.

CHLO: *(as GARTH)* No.

SAGE: When I walked down the street today, men looked.

CHLO: *(as GARTH)* They always look.

SAGE: That's because I dress weird. But today it was a sexual look.

CHLO: *(as GARTH)* You can tell the difference?

SAGE: Garth, I'm slightly psychic. I ought to know the difference between "Oh my God, get a load of that wacko!" and "Hm. I'd like to melt the mascara off that bitch."

CHLO: *(as GARTH)* Sage, will you marry me?

SAGE: Chlo, don't make him ask me that.

CHLO: Look. I'm trying to feel the way he feels based on what I know about him.

GRACE: Sage, Garth asked you a question.

SAGE: I'm sorry, Grace. I can't do this.

GRACE: Why?

SAGE: Because Garth will not ask me to marry him. It's not in the cards.

GRACE: I thought it was very incisive of Chlo to ask you. Why don't you answer?

SAGE: Why answer a question that will never be asked? And I feel Chlo's love stronger than Garth's and that makes me confused ... depressed ... No, confused.

GRACE: Do you want to marry Garth?

SAGE: I've asked him.

LIZ: Ask again tonight.

CHLO: And if he says no, then marry me.

LIZ: Chlo, why would you say that?

CHLO: Oh. I'm just joking. You know that.

LIZ: Could there be an element of truth underneath?

CHLO: Hey, lay off. I'm just easing the tension.

LIZ: What tension?

CHLO: The sexual tension.

LIZ: What sexual tension? I don't feel any sexual tension. Do you feel any sexual tension!?

MOLLY: Uh ... no.

DENA: A little.

SAGE: Maybe sexual confusion.

CHLO: I feel it. You're all threatened by me.

LIZ: I don't think so. Because we know you're not serious.

CHLO: How do you know that?

LIZ: How long has it been since you've had a lover?

CHLO: Liz, lay off. Grace?

GRACE: I'd say go on. Answer her.

CHLO: You guys know I can't with Travis. He'd –

LIZ: Excuse!

CHLO: Damn good one.

LIZ: *(Crossing to Chlo)* Let's play this out, Chlo. You be you and I'll be me and I'll say, "Yes." Wanna try?

CHLO: Don't be ridiculous.

LIZ: I'm serious.

SAGE: Go for it, Chlo.

MOLLY: Yeah.

LIZ: Join me in Paris next week. I've got so many mileage points, they're going to expire.

CHLO: Paris? *(Beat)* Moi?

LIZ: It's the most romantic city in the world.

CHLO: Yeah. Maybe I'd meet someone.

LIZ: Maybe you have.

(She takes Chlo's hand.)

CHLO: Oh, Liz. *(She pulls away)* Don't.

LIZ: It scares you, doesn't it?

CHLO: Of course it does. Don't do this to me.

LIZ: What scares you the most? That I would hurt you or that you might get into a relationship?

CHLO: Forget it. Just forget it.

LIZ: You're terrified of falling in love with anyone of any sex. You're scared shitless of getting hurt and you use Travis as your "damn good" excuse, but that's all it is –

CHLO: Tons of single mothers feel that way.

LIZ: So, stop flirting here where it's safe. Flirt where it's dangerous, with someone who might take you up on it.

CHLO: You think you're so smart, that you know all about me and my family and just what I should do.

(MUSIC BEGINS.)

CHLO: But .... This has nothing to do with Travis. And you don't know me.

SONG: "NEVER ENOUGH" *(CHLO)*

CHLO:
I HAVE HAD SOME LOVERS IN MY PAST,
AND SOME HAVE HAD ME,
JUST WHEN I THINK, THIS ONE'S GOING TO LAST,
THEY WANT TO BE FREE.

I KNOW WHY THEY GO AWAY,
THEY SEE MY HUNGER AND THEY RUN,
I SMOTHER THEM WITH OVERBEARING LOVE,
THEY FIND OUT VERY SOON
THAT ALL THE LOVE I GET IS NEVER ENOUGH.

WHEN I NEED A LOVER'S TOUCH,
I SIMPLY LOSE MY NERVE,
I START TO THINK, I'M ASKING FOR TOO MUCH,
MORE THAN I DESERVE.
WHY EVEN TAKE A CHANCE?
IT'S NEVER GOING TO LAST.
THE PAIN OF STARTING OVER GETS TOO ROUGH
SO I'VE STOPPED STARTING OVER
`CAUSE ALL THE LOVE I GET IS NEVER ENOUGH.

WHEN I FALL IN LOVE
I LOVE TO BE BESIDE YOU,
CURL UP AGAINST YOUR BODY
EVERY MORNING, EVERY NIGHT.
I LONG TO HEAR YOUR DREAMS
AND CALM THE FEARS INSIDE YOU
AND PAINT YOUR PICTURE
IN THE BEAUTY OF THE LATE AFTERNOON LIGHT.

I KNOW EVERY TIME I FLIRT,
I'M HIDING WHAT I FEEL,
THE TIMES I SEEM TO GET HURT
ARE WHEN I'M BEING REAL.
WHEN WILL I FIND SOMEONE
WHO WANTS ME AS I AM
WHO SEES MY GAME AND CALLS MY BLUFF?
`TIL THAT LOVER COMES ALONG
THE LOVE I GET WILL NEVER BE ENOUGH.

GRACE: That's wonderful, Chlo. It's so important that you've allowed yourself to work on what you need.

SAGE: Whoa. As long as I've been your group-mate, I

always thought you were like this gay ... nun. I'm so happy that you've shown us this awesome side of your prism and look at you! If you could see your aura now, you'd shit.

GRACE: Ooh. We've gone overtime.

SAGE: *(As she exits)* Really. It's breathtaking.

GRACE: And we need to clear out.

MOLLY: I think I know a lady who'd like to meet you. Should I have her call you? *(CHLO thinks, then nods)* You're a real catch, you know that, don't you?

(They embrace and MOLLY exits.)

LIZ: Chlo, I'm sorry if I pushed you too far. Are you okay? *(CHLO nods)* I feel like we're not done here, that you've just started. Can we go get coffee or ... ?

CHLO: I have to go back to work. Don't you?!

LIZ: Yes, but I'd be willing to re-shuffle.

CHLO: I'll be fine. Thank you ... especially.

(LIZ embraces CHLO, then exits.)

DENA: It's been a long time for me, but what you said, it was like you were saying it for me. I'm the same way.

CHLO: What!?

DENA: No. I mean with men.

CHLO: Oh, gorgeous, I knew that's what you meant.

(They exit.)

SONG: Scene Change 5

(GRACE re-positions the chairs. The OTHERS re-enter. SAGE is not as dressed up as before.)

LIZ: *(To DENA)* How are the rehearsals coming?

DENA: Good. The music director and I get along great. We –

LIZ & CHLO & MOLLY: Truth!

DENA: It's hell! But I'm getting there. It'll be there.

CHLO: Doing any new songs?

DENA: Yes. As a matter of fact, I'm doing one new song ... a song I wrote.

LIZ: Great! What's it called?

DENA: "Reaching Up."

MOLLY: I'm so excited.

CHLO: Me, too. The drop's almost done.

MOLLY: Sage, are you okay?

GRACE: You look like you've seen a ghost.

(SAGE shakes her head trying to fight back her tears.)

CHLO: What's the matter?

SAGE: Nothing. I just feel like I'm not contributing anything to Dena's cabaret.

DENA: You made the flyers and those book-mark ticket things.

LIZ: That's not it.

DENA: Is it Garth?

SAGE: He's away on a business trip.

MOLLY: Did you put white light around him?

SAGE: *(Beat)* No.

LIZ: Why not?

SAGE: He's a materialistic phony. He doesn't deserve the energy it takes to put white light around him.

LIZ: Uh oh.

CHLO: Does this mean proposal #2 didn't fly?

SAGE: I have nothing to say.

MOLLY: You never say anything anyway.

SAGE: Yes I do!?

MOLLY: When?

LIZ: Grace always has to push you.

DENA: What happened when you proposed again?

SAGE: Nothing.

MOLLY: Nothing?

DENA: Come on, Sage.

SAGE: He laughed.

MOLLY: Creep.

SAGE: He laughed and laughed and I tried not to get mad.
GRACE: But you were mad.
SAGE: I still am. He's married.
CHLO: Bastard!
DENA: Lowlife.
SAGE: They've been separated for years.
LIZ: Clever.
DENA: What did you say to him?
SAGE: Nothing. I just stared.
ALL: Why?
SAGE: Because that's me, I never ...

(MUSIC BEGINS.)

SAGE: I just ...

SONG: "I DON'T SAY ANYTHING"   *(SAGE)*

SAGE:
I SAY SOMETHING IS OKAY
WHEN IT'S REALLY NOT OKAY,
I SAY EVERYTHING IS FINE,
I DON'T MAKE WAVES.
YOU LIKE THAT RESTAURANT FOR DINNER?
THAT'S WHERE WE'RE GOING TO GO.
IT'S AMAZING ...
HOW MUCH ARGUMENT IT SAVES.

I PUT ASIDE MY PROBLEMS
TO HELP EVERYBODY ELSE,
I DO ANYTHING THAT ANYBODY WANTS.
I HAVE CANCELED THREE VACATIONS
TO HELP SOMEBODY MOVE,
I GIVE UP DREAMS WITH TOTAL NONCHALANCE.

I DON'T SAY ANYTHING
WORTHWHILE.
I DON'T SAY ANYTHING,

I SMILE.
SEE HOW I GIVE UP WHAT I WANT
SO YOU DON'T FEEL BAD?
I DON'T SAY ANYTHING,
BUT I'M MAD.

WHEN MY GURU SAID, "EAT THIS."
AND I SWEAR IT SMELLED LIKE SHIT.
I SAID, "WELL, OKAY, I'LL EAT IT,
YOU KNOW BEST."
WHEN MY TRAINER TOLD ME "BEND,"
AND I KNEW I COULDN'T "BEND"
I SAID, "SURE,"
AND THEN FOR WEEKS I WAS A MESS.

WHEN MY LOVING BOYFRIEND, GARTH,
ATE MY LIMA BEAN SOUFFLÉ
AND SAID HIS WIFE WOULDN'T GIVE HIM A DIVORCE.
I'LL GIVE HIM UP, NO PROBLEM.
WHY EVEN TRY TO FIGHT?
HAD TO GIVE HER WHAT SHE WANTS, OF COURSE.

DID NOT SAY ANYTHING
ASTUTE.
DID NOT SAY ANYTHING
I WAS MUTE.
SEE HOW I TURN THE OTHER CHEEK
WHEN MY ASS GETS KICKED?
I DON'T SAY ANYTHING
BUT I'M TICKED!

WHY SHOULD I OFFER MY OPINION?
DO I HAVE MY OWN OPINION?
HOW DO I KNOW WHAT I'M FEELING IS OKAY?
WHY SHOULD I ASK FOR WHAT I WANT
WHEN I KNOW THAT WHAT I WANT
I WILL NEVER GET ANYWAY.

IT'S SO CRAZY TO SAY YES
WHEN YOUR HEART'S NOT SAYING YES,
BUT IT'S EASIER TO SAY IT
THAN TO NOT,
IF I ONLY HAD SOME SATURN
TO DISCIPLINE MY LIFE
I WOULD NOT GIVE UP
EVERYTHING I'VE GOT.

I SAY, "HERE, PLEASE TAKE MY SOUL."
I SAY, "REALLY, NO BIG DEAL."
I SAY, "WHAT I NEED CAN WAIT ANOTHER DAY."
I SAY, "GO ON, YOU PICK THIS TIME."
I SAY, "MY LIFE'S NOT IMPORTANT."
I SAY LOTS OF THINGS I SAY I SAY I SAY.

I DON'T SAY ANYTHING
AT ALL.
I DON'T SAY ANYTHING
I CRAWL.
SEE HOW I FIT INTO YOUR PLANS
AS IF MINE DID NOT EXIST?
SEE HOW I DO NOT SEEM TO CARE
THERE'S A LIFE I'VE MISSED?
SEE HOW MY VOICE IS SMOOTH AND CALM
THOUGH MY HAND IS IN A FIST?
I DON'T SAY ANYTHING
BUT I'M PISSED!

(They ALL cheer for SAGE.)

GRACE: Good work, Sage.
SAGE: Thank you, Grace. Was that a little breakthrough?
GRACE: Only if it sticks when you walk out that door.
SAGE: It will.
MOLLY: And next time, if you can't say anything, try kicking.
DENA: So you'll tell Garth: "no divorce, no dates."

SAGE: No.

ALL: Sage!

SAGE: Well, I could never say that so Readers' Digesty. I'd have to explain and –

LIZ: Say it more National Geographic-ally.

SAGE: *(Thinks)* Yeah.

LIZ: Okay. So, do it the minute you get home.

SAGE: How can I call him up and say: "no divorce, no date" when we don't even have a date tonight? He'll never ask me out again! *(SILENCE. SAGE looks around at all the knowing smiles)* Oh. That would be okay though, wouldn't it. *(They ALL nod)* Just call him up? *(Beat)* I will.

MOLLY: Speaking of divorce, I have an announcement.

CHLO: Oh, no.

MOLLY: Since Harry moved out, I've lost five pounds.

DENA: Oh, Molly.

MOLLY: Yeah. It's the old divorce diet. Actually we're trying a separation first. I'm letting him go live with the other woman to get it out of his system.

LIZ: There is another woman?

MOLLY: Yeah. But I'm relieved and I actually met her. Can you believe I'm being so civilized?

SAGE: See? You have this quiet, earthly strength you didn't even know you had. And more where that came from.

DENA: How can you be so calm about it?

MOLLY: I'm not, I ... did all my suffering before he moved out.

GRACE: Do you want to work – ?

MOLLY: No. *(Beat)* But I have prepared a little funeral ceremony for my marriage certificate.

(MUSIC BEGINS.)

SONG: "THE PASSING OF A FRIEND"
   (MOLLY & COMPANY)

MOLLY:
WE ARE GATHERED HERE TODAY

TO MOURN THE PASSING OF A FRIEND.
IT'S SAD TO SAY GOOD-BYE,
BUT ALL GOOD THINGS MUST END.
AS WE LAY THIS MARRIAGE DOWN
IN ITS FINAL RESTING PLACE,
LET US BURY IT FOREVER
WITH SOME PIOUS WORDS OF GRACE.

GOOD-BYE, MARRIAGE.
HELLO, HAPPINESS.
GOODBYE, MARRIAGE.
AMEN. ·GOD BLESS.
I'VE NEVER BEEN TO HEAVEN
BUT NOW THAT YOU ARE GONE,
I'VE GOT A BETTER CHANCE THAN EVER,
AND I'M GONNA CARRY, CARRY ON.

YOU'RE A STUPID PIECE OF PAPER,
I KNOW YOU WERE NEVER REAL.
JUST A BUNCH OF LEGAL WORDS
THAT NEVER SAID THE WAY I FEEL.
FROM NOW ON I'M SIGNING NOTHING
TIL I RE-LEARN HOW TO TRUST.
ASHES TO ASHES, AND DUST, I SAID DUST, TO DUST.
SING IT WITH ME NOW!

MOLLY:	OTHER:
	GOODBYE, MARRIAGE,
HELLO, HAPPINESS.	
AMEN. GOD BLESS.	
I'VE NEVER BEEN	
TO HEAVEN	OO HOO
BUT NOW THAT YOU	
ARE GONE,	HOO HOO
I'VE GOT A BETTER CHANCE	
THAN EVER	HOO
I'M GONNA CARRY,	
CARRY ON	CARRY ON. CARRY ON.

GOODBYE, MARRIAGE,	GOODBYE,
HELLO, HAPPINESS	I SAID GOODBYE.
(I SAID GOODBYE)	
GOODBYE, MARRIAGE,	GOODBYE,
AMEN. GOD BLESS.	I SAID GOODBYE.
(I SAID GOODBYE)	
I'VE NEVER BEEN	I'VE NEVER,
TO HEAVEN	TO HEAVEN,
(GOODBYE, GOODBYE)	

BUT NOW THAT   BUT NOW THAT
   YOU ARE GONE   YOU ARE GONE
   (GOODBYE, GOODBYE, GOODBYE)
I'VE GOT A BETTER CHANCE GLORY, GLORY
   THAN EVER   HALLELUJAH
   (HALLELUJAH)
AND I'M GONNA CARRY,   CARRY ON,
   CARRY ON.   CARRY ON.

MOLLY, GRACE, DENA:	**SAGE, LIZ, CHLO:**
GOODBYE MARRIAGE	GOODBYE,
HELLO, HAPPINESS	I SAID GOODBYE
GOODBYE MARRIAGE	GOODBYE,
AMEN, GOD BLESS.	I SAID GOODBYE.
I'M PICKING MYSELF UP	OOH
GONNA FACE	OOH
A BRAND NEW DAWN,	
I'M GONNA ...	
KISS OFF HARRY,	*(Spoken)* Yeah!
KISS OFF HARRY,	*(Spoken)* Yeah!

   ALL:
KISS OFF, HARRY
AND I'M GONNA CARRY ON!

   LIZ: Molly, you sure you don't want to work?
   MOLLY: I'm sure.

(She sits down.)

LIZ: I've decided to take the job.

(Scattered CHEERS.)

CHLO: Why?

LIZ: This is an opportunity of a lifetime. I'll hate myself –

DENA: Have you told Ron?

LIZ: I was going to last night when he launched a sneak attack of his own. He wants me to budget my time and include a minimum amount of family time each five-day work-week.

MOLLY: He must really love you.

LIZ: *(As she distributes copies)* I made copies for everyone.

CHLO: She's so organized. It's just like being at a condo board meeting.

SAGE: *(Studying schedule)* All your solo time is shot to shit. When do you get to meditate?

MOLLY: He's only allowing you 20 hours of family time?

LIZ: He's only asking for 20 hours on the work-week. And I can't even handle that much.

DENA: But won't the new job allow you shorter hours?

LIZ: It might. It's flexible, but I'll be gone on long trips.

MOLLY: Talk to Ron.

GRACE: You've put it off so long. Do you want to practice?

LIZ: No.

GRACE: Come on. Pick a 'Ron', any 'Ron'.

LIZ: I really – *(CHLO stands up)* Okay. I'll be Ron.

GRACE: And I'll be you.

(GRACE and LIZ step away from the group. LIZ [As RON] assumes a slouched position.)

GRACE: *(As LIZ)* I got a job offer.

LIZ: *(As RON)* What, you'd take a second job?

GRACE: *(As LIZ)* A new job, a better job, my dream job.

LIZ: *(As RON)* Really? What perfect timing. Will they wait four months?

GRACE: *(As LIZ)* No.

LIZ: *(As RON)* Next month I start my apprenticeship. You know how long it took to set it up and –

GRACE: *(As LIZ)* You can! We'll get a live-in maid.

LIZ: *(As RON)* To take the place of our live-out mother?

GRACE: *(As LIZ)* Ron. Can you please try and see –

LIZ: *(As RON)* Liz, I think it's great that you're so successful. Hats off! But I'm still here at the starting gate choking on your dust. When I go train to be a chef, the kids will come home to no one. They need at least one parent here; to talk to, to depend on.

GRACE: *(As LIZ)* I'll be able to give them more quality time, when I'm in town.

LIZ: *(As RON)* They don't need an occasionally super mom, they need a consistently present mom.

GRACE: *(As LIZ)* I'll work on it. Ron, this is the chance of a lifetime and –

LIZ: *(As RON)* No! Liz, your pattern is too clear. You'll have to impress the new boss. You'll stay late, you'll stay over, you'll stay away. *(Beat)* You know, I do a lot of thinking when I'm here alone. And I wonder if we're making each other unhappy.

GRACE: *(As LIZ)* I hope not.

LIZ: *(As RON)* And I think, "I'm running this household, alone. I could divorce you, get custody and you'd only have to worry about one big bill each month. How simple our lives would be –

(She stops. MUSIC BEGINS.)

SONG: "THINGS LOOK DIFFERENT" *(LIZ & GRACE)*

LIZ:
OH, GOD, DID I SAY THAT?
IS THAT WHAT I'M THINKING DOWN DEEP?
I CAN'T BELIEVE THAT WAS ME,
IT WAS SOMEONE ELSE TALKING...
WHILE I WAS ASLEEP.

CHLO: *(Spoken)* No. It was you.

MOLLY: *(Spoken)* And it was Ron.
GRACE: *(Spoken)* How do you feel?
LIZ:
STANDING IN HIS SHOES, SEEING THROUGH HIS EYES,
THINGS LOOK DIFFERENT.
GRACE:
THEY ALWAYS DO.
LIZ:
DO I SEEM CONFUSED? WHAT A DAMN SURPRISE!
THINGS LOOK DIFFERENT.
GRACE:
I KNOW. IT'S TRUE.
LIZ:
HAVE I STAYED AWAY TOO MUCH?
WILL HE CALL IT QUITS?
I'VE BEEN OUT OF TOUCH
AND DIDN'T SEE THINGS FROM WHERE HE SITS.
GRACE:
OF COURSE, YOU DIDN'T.
BUT NOW YOU DO.
LIZ:
SITTING IN HIS CHAIR, SAYING ALL HIS LINES,
THINGS LOOK DIFFERENT.
GRACE:
TELL US HOW.
LIZ:
HAVE I BEEN UNFAIR? HAVE I BEEN UNKIND?
I CAN BE DIFFERENT.
GRACE:
AND NOW?
LIZ:
I WILL TURN THE OFFER DOWN,
BE MORE OF A MOM,
SPEND MORE TIME IN TOWN ... *(SHE LAUGHS)*.
THIS ISN'T RIGHT FOR ME,
IT'S GONNA BLOW UP LIKE A BOMB.
GRACE:
WAIT A MINUTE, JUST A MINUTE,

YOU WERE STANDING IN HIS SHOES,
SEEING THROUGH HIS EYES ...
    LIZ:
I CAN DO THIS.
    GRACE:
HOW DO YOU KNOW?
    LIZ:
I CAN TAKE THE JOB.
HE CAN BE A CHEF.
WE CAN DO THIS.
    GRACE:
YOU THINK? HOW SO?
    LIZ:
THE CHILDREN WILL ADJUST.
WE'LL FIND THE EXTRA TIME,
I'LL MAKE DECENT MONEY
WHICH THE KIDS WILL NEED FOR COLLEGE ...
    GRACE:
YOU ARE MISSING THE ISSUE.
    LIZ:
NO! THIS IS THE ISSUE:
BEHIND EVERY SUCCESSFUL MAN
THERE IS A WOMAN WHO HELPS HIM PLAY THE GAME,
BEHIND EVERY SUCCESSFUL WOMAN
THERE OUGHT TO BE A MAN WHO DOES THE SAME.
    GRACE:
HE'S BEEN BEHIND YOU ALL THE WAY.
LOOK INSIDE HIS HEART, LOOK INSIDE HIS HEAD,
IS HE FEELING KIND OF GRIM?
    LIZ:
YES, HE IS.
    GRACE:
CAN YOU SEE HIS THOUGHTS?
WHAT DO YOU BELIEVE
HE WOULD WANT YOU TO SAY ... TO HIM?
    LIZ:
(TO AN IMAGINARY RON) IF YOU PROPOSE DIVORCE,
IT WILL BREAK MY HEART FOREVER,

IF WE CAN TALK IT OUT,
WE CAN MAKE THINGS BETTER.
I DON'T WANT TO LOSE YOU,
NOT NOW, NOT EVER ...
OPEN YOUR ARMS, I'M COMING IN,
HOLD ME AS CLOSE AS YOU CAN BEAR,
LET'S SEE HOW DIFFERENT
THINGS LOOK FROM THERE.

LIZ: Why is life so difficult?

DENA: Difficult? Two prestigious companies want you to work for them, you have a wonderful husband and family. Everybody wants your time. We should all have such hard choices.

LIZ: I'm sure there was a time when different record companies wanted you and you had to choose. That's where I am. I want to make the right decision so I don't end up like you. *(Wincing at what she said)* Sorry.

CHLO: Oh, shut up, Liz. You could walk in anywhere.

LIZ: Today, yes. If I make a wrong move, in three months, no.

DENA: Okay, then. Let's reverse. What would you do if you were in my position?

LIZ: I'd spend every waking second pumping energy into that show. I'd make certain the record people were going to be there – even if it meant hiring a limo.

DENA: And what if it didn't work? What then?

LIZ: Don't think that way. Concentrate on the cabaret. This is your immediate goal and nothing should deter you.

MOLLY: That's good advice, Dena.

SAGE: Yeah. And she didn't even charge you.

GRACE: Dena, what would you do if you were in Liz's shoes?

DENA: Me? I'd stop plucking my eyebrows so severely.

CHLO: Yea!! Someone finally told her!

SAGE: I thought they grew that way. You pluck them?

LIZ: My eyebrows are hideous. I look like a caveman if I don't control them.

DENA: Really Liz, what I actually think you should –

LIZ: I know. Keep the job, save the family that's because you don't have –

DENA: Hold it. Do you want me to answer or do you want to stuff an answer down my throat so I can regurgitate it back to you?

SAGE: Yeah. Go, Dena!

DENA: My first inclination was, in fact, to tell you to take the new job. Because you're right. Had I gone with the new label, I might have done better, but I stayed. *(Beat)* So, if I were you, I'd start my own company. Why work that hard and that long for someone else, when you could put the money in your own pocket?

LIZ: You are such a romantic. I can't just set up a –

DENA: They're dangling candy in front of you. Go for protein.

CHLO: Think about it, Liz.

LIZ: Shit.

MOLLY: Now what.

LIZ: Now I have a third option. It would be so simple to just take the candy.

(MUSIC BEGINS.)

SONG: "DO IT AT HOME" *(ALL)*

DENA:
DO IT AT HOME,
BE YOUR OWN BOSS,
WITH AN OFFICE AT HOME
YOU WON'T HAVE TO TREK DOWNTOWN.
CHLO:
A MAHOGANY DESK
IN YOUR STUDY,
AN EXECUTIVE CHAIR
ONE OF MY PAINTINGS – THERE!
SAGE:
A VELVET COUCH FOR CLIENTS.
MOLLY: *(Spoken)* Chocolate brown?

GRACE:	OTHERS:
DO IT AT HOME	DOO WAH
WHERE IT'S COMFY	DOO WAH
YOU SET UP A PHONE	DOO WAH
YOU PUT A FEW BOOKS	
ON A SHELF	
SOME PENCILS AND PENS,	DOO WAH
A COMPUTER,	AHH HAH

MOLLY:	OTHERS:
LIFE WILL BE SWEET,	LIFE WILL BE SWEET,
THE WORLD AT YOUR FEET,	YOUR FEET,
A COMPANY THAT YOU	OOH HOO
CAN LEAD YOURSELF.	YOURSELF.

ALL:
NO TRAV'LING TO DO
UNLESS IT'S FOR YOU.
YOU'LL BE SO IN DEMAND
THEY'LL STAND IN LINE
   TO GET THROUGH.

SAGE:	OTHERS:
RON WILL BE SO AMAZED,	AMAZED

MOLLY:	
THE KIDS WILL BE CRAZED,	BE CRAZED

ALL:
YOU WILL HAVE YOUR CAKE
AND EAT IT TOO!

CHLO:	OTHERS:
YOU CAN DO IT AT HOME	OH, YEAH
AT ANY HOUR,	OH, YEAH
AT FIVE O'CLOCK	OH, YEAH
WHEN THE REST OF THE	
WORLD'S DRIVING HOME.	

DENA:
RON WILL MAKE
   SALMON MOUSSE   DOO WAH
WHILE YOU'RE TALKING
   TO LONDON   AHH HAH
   GRACE:
YOU'LL GET ALL
   YOUR WORK DONE   *(Spoken)* Yeah.
STILL HAVE TIME
   FOR FUN.   *(Spoken)* Yeah.
   MOLLY:
YOU AND RON CAN PLAN
A DREAM TRIP TO ROME!
   SAGE: *(Spoken)* At the same time!

LIZ:	**OTHERS:**
I DON'T KNOW IF I CAN	YOU CAN
BE MY OWN MAN	YOU CAN
THE VERY IDEA	DO DO DO
MAKES ME	DO DO DO
SHORT OF BREATH	AHH
MY OWN LIVELIHOOD,	YOUR OWN
IT SOUNDS GOOD.	AT HOME
BUT I'VE GOT TO ADMIT	
IT SCARES ME	
HALF TO DEATH	HALF TO DEATH
	DO IT AT HOME
DOO WAH	NO MORE OFFICE
DOO WAH	BALLYHOO IT
	AT HOME
DOO WAH	I KNOW YOU CAN
	MAKE IT GO.
	RON WILL BE A CHEF
(Spoken) Oh, yeah.	YOU'LL HAVE YOUR
	OWN BUSINESS.
(Spoken) Uh-huh.	HE'LL BE ROLLING
	IN YEAST,
	YOUR PALM WILL
	BE GREASED.

ONE VOICE: *(Deep)*
AND YOU BOTH WILL BE
KNEE-DEEP ... IN DOUGH.   KNEE-DEEP IN DOUGH!
    ONE VOICE: *(Deep)*
OOH WEE-EE-EE-HEE

(LIGHTS FADE on circle.)

SONG: Scene Change 6

(LIGHTS COME UP on a single chair, which will indicate a make-up mirror and dressing table in a dressing room. LIZ, CHLO and MOLLY enter wearing slightly dressier clothes.)

CHLO: How does it look out there?
MOLLY: Good. It's filling up. How's she doing?
LIZ: Okay. I think she'll be fine once she gets started.
MOLLY: Hey, Chlo. Did my friend ever call you?
CHLO: Oh, yeah. She did.
LIZ: And?
CHLO: And she was very nice.
MOLLY: So?
CHLO: It didn't ... escalate, but she referred me to a friend who needed some water colors for a presentation.
LIZ: She liked your paintings?
CHLO: And the sculpture ... and Travis ... and me.
MOLLY: Really?
CHLO: Yes. Is that so hard to believe?
MOLLY: No. It just makes me feel so good to have helped in a small way.

(DENA enters wearing a bathrobe over a beautiful dress.)

DENA: How did I ever let you guys talk me into this?
CHLO: What's the hold-up, beautiful?
DENA: I'm just waiting for everyone to get here. Is Mom okay?
LIZ: She's having a ball. Should I do jokes?

DENA: No. I want them to stay.

(GRACE and SAGE enter, also dressier.)

GRACE: What's wrong? Everyone is getting restless.
MOLLY: Some of the record people are actually here.
SAGE: And lots of other fans.
DENA: Oh, God.
GRACE: *(To DENA)* You okay?
DENA: No. I want to disappear.
CHLO: No. You need to reappear.
LIZ: I'm going to tell them to start the music. We're going to take our seats and you'd better goddam be up there and sing your heart out. Come on, girls, let's –
DENA: No! I ... I can't. It's too ... My nerves are ... I must've had too much coffee ...
MOLLY: Hey. What's all this?
CHLO: You've done this hundreds of times.
DENA: Not in the last ...
GRACE: Are you warmed up?
DENA: Well, yes. We had a soundcheck at four, but – I don't know if I can do this, you guys. It's not like going out there the first time.
LIZ: It's harder. We know.

(MOLLY steps up and squeezes DENA's hand.)

MOLLY: You can do it.
DENA: They all have such high expectations.

(MUSIC BEGINS.)

SONG: "REACHING UP" *(DENA & COMPANY)*

DENA:
DO I HAVE IT IN ME TO START OVER AGAIN?
HAS MY MOMENT GONE BY?
IS IT TOO LATE TO TRY?

DO I WANT TO WALK INTO THAT SPOTLIGHT AGAIN?
SHOW THEM ALL HOW I SHINE?
LAY MY SOUL ON THE LINE?

IS MY LIFE IN MUSIC JUST A DREAM THAT'S GONE?
DID SOMEBODY PLAY A JOKE ON ME?
AM I JUST A FOOL TO THINK OF GOING ON,
TRYING TO BE SOMEONE I USED TO BE?

(During the next, MOLLY stands up and starts to remove Dena's bathrobe, revealing a beautiful evening gown. LIZ stands up and positions DENA a little more comfortably. LIZ hands CHLO some rhinestone barrettes. CHLO places the barrettes in DENA's hair. They stand back and survey their handiwork, then sit down again.)

REACHING UP,
WONDERING WHO I AM
WAITING FOR A DRUM
OR SOME TELEGRAM.
REACHING UP,
LOOKING FOR A SPACE,
SOMEWHERE IN THIS WORLD
WHERE I HAVE A PLACE.

(DENA becomes more comfortable now and takes stage.)

TIRED OF WANTING WHAT WILL NEVER BE AGAIN,
NOTHING'S GAINED FROM LIVING IN THE PAST.
WHAT DO I HAVE NOW THAT I DID NOT HAVE THEN?
IS THERE SOMETHING GOOD THAT'S GONNA LAST?

REACHING UP,
ON THIS EMPTY STAGE,
TIME TO MOVE AHEAD, TURN ANOTHER PAGE.

(As DENA gets caught up in the song, the LIGHTS CHANGE to suggest what her show would actually look like onstage. She is beautifully backlit and a follow-spot hits her from the front. She comes alive.)

REACHING UP,
MAYBE I WILL FALL,
BUT I HAVE LEARNED TO LAND
AND STILL STAND UP TALL.

I'M NO LONGER TWENTY,
WHAT A DAMN SURPRISE!
MAYBE THAT'S A BLESSING IN DISGUISE.
MAYBE DOORS WILL OPEN, MAYBE DOORS WILL SHUT,
SHOOT FOR THE MOON –
NO MATTER WHAT!
REACHING UP.

GOTTA TAKE MY CHANCES AND JUST DO IT.
BETTER THAN I'VE EVER DONE BEFORE.
IF I FIND THE STRENGTH TO GET ME THROUGH IT,
I'LL BE DOING WHAT I LOVE ONCE MORE.

REACHING UP,
HIGH AS I CAN SEE,
GOTTA CLEAR THE CLOUDS
HANGING OVER ME.
REACHING UP,
HIGHER THAN THE SKY,
GONNA LISTEN TO MY HEART
AND LET THE MUSIC FLY.

(The other women jump in.)

ALL:
GOTTA TAKE MY CHANCES AND JUST DO IT.
BETTER THAN I'VE EVER DONE BEFORE.
IF I FIND THE STRENGTH TO GET ME THROUGH IT,
I'LL BE DOING WHAT I LOVE ONCE MORE.
AND MORE! *(AND MORE)*

REACHING UP,
HIGH AS I CAN SEE,

GOTTA CLEAR THE CLOUDS HANGING OVER ME.
REACHING UP,
THAT'S WHERE I BELONG,
GONNA LISTEN TO MY HEART *(GONNA LISTEN TO MY HEART)*
AND SING A BRAND NEW SONG.

(CURTAIN.)

Other Publications for Your Interest

THE ACT
(LITTLE THEATRE—MUSICAL)
Book by GEORGE FURTH
Music by JOHN KANDER
Lyrics by FRED EBB

5 men, 2 women
plus male & female ensemble - one set

Liza Minelli took Broadway by storm in this "concept musical" about a Las Vegas night-club performer named Michelle Craig, a has-been movie star now trying to make a comeback. All the terrific Kander and Ebb songs are sung by Michelle, making this an amazing tour de force for your best female musical performer. "A striking and intense show...an ambitious and big time musical with terrific entertainment values and stage excitement."—N.Y. Post. *"The Act* is precisely what its name implies; it is an act, and a splendid one."—N.Y. Times. (Terms quoted on application. Music available on Rental.)
(#3913)

ANGRY HOUSEWIVES
(LITTLE THEATRE—MUSICAL)
Book & Lyrics by A.M. COLLINS
Music & Lyrics by CHAD HENRY

4 men, 4 women - various sets

Bored with their everyday, workaday lives and kept in insignificance by their boyfriends/husbands—these really are four *angry* housewives. They try a number of things in search of personal fulfillment, but nothing strikes a chord until one of them strikes a chord on her guitar, and gets the idea that, well, why don't they form a punk-rock group and enter the upcoming talent show down at the neighborhood punk club? Of course they form the group, of course they enter, and of course they win, calling themselves—of course—"The Angry Housewives", winning the contest—and stopping the show—with their punk-rock song "Eating Your F***ing Cornflakes!" This genial satire of contemporary feminism ran for ages in Seattle, and has had numerous successful productions cross-country. "The show is insistently outrageous, frequently funny, occasionally witty and altogether irresistible."—Seattle Times. (Terms quoted on application. Music available on Rental.) (Slightly Restricted.Posters)

(#3931)

Other Publications for Your Interest

OLYMPUS ON MY MIND
(ALL GROUPS—MUSICAL)
Book & Lyrics by BARRY HARMAN
Music by GRANT STURIALE

6 men, 3 women—Exterior

This delightful new Broadway hit recalls the good old days of Broadway musicals such as *The Boys from Syracuse*. Based on the Amphitryon myth, "Olympus" is about what happens when Jupiter decides to come to Earth in human form, there to bed the beautiful Alcmene, wife of Amphitryon. Jupiter appears to Alcmene in the body of her absent husband, and quickly wins her love. Things go swimmingly for old Jove; until, that is, the *real* Amphitryon shows up. Also along for the ride is Mercury, Jupiter's servant—who appears in the guise of Amphitryon's servant to woo Alcmene's handmaiden. And, there is a chorus: Tom, Dick and Horace, augmented by the delightfully dizzy Dolores (who is only in the show because she is the wife of its financial backer, Murray the Furrier; and who makes every appearance wearing a different fur from Murray's impressive stock—even when it is totally inappropriate to the show, which is most of the time!) "Percolates with an old-fashioned sense of naughty musical comedy fun."—NY Times. "A dazzling musical spoof...bouncing music and witty lyrics."—Newsday. "Diverting & frisky...never less than fun."

(#165)

THE TAP DANCE KID
(ALL GROUPS—MUSICAL)
Book by CHARLES BLACKWELL
Music by HENRY KRIEGER
Lyrics by ROBERT LORICK

5 men, 5 women
plus ensemble - various sets

Based on the novel "Nobody's Family's Going to Change" by Louise Fitzhugh. This long-running Broadway musical also had a lengthy and successful tour. It's a wonderful cornucopia of music, drama, comedy, and above all, tap-dancing. The story concerns a 10 year-old Black kid named Willie who doesn't *want* to be a lawyer like his stern father; Willie just has to *dance*, like his uncle, an aspiring Broadway choreographer who is very much Willie's mentor. And, dance he does! "Stunning, warm-hearted new musical comedy."—Christian Science Monitor.

(#22617)

Other Publications for Your Interest

A . . . MY NAME IS ALICE
(LITTLE THEATRE—REVUE)
Conceived by JOAN MICKLIN SILVER and JULIANNE BOYD

5 women—Bare stage with set pieces

This terrific new show definitely rates an "A"—in fact, an "A-*plus*"! Originally produced by the Women's Project at the American Place Theatre in New York City, "Alice" settled down for a long run at the Village Gate, off Broadway. When you hear the songs, and read the sketches, you'll know why. The music runs the gamut from blues to torch to rock to wistful easy listening. There are hilarious songs, such as "Honeypot" (about a Black blues singer who can only sing about sex euphemistically) and heartbreakingly beautiful numbers such as "I Sure Like the Boys". A . . . *My Name Is Alice* is a feminist revue in the best sense. It could charm even the most die-hard male chauvinist. "Delightful . . . the music and lyrics are so sophisticated that they can carry the weight of one-act plays".—NY Times. "Bright, party-time, pick-me-up stuff . . . Bouncy music, witty patter, and a bundle of laughs".—NY Post.   (#3647)

I'M GETTING MY ACT TOGETHER AND TAKING IT ON THE ROAD
(ALL GROUPS—MUSICAL)
Book and Lyrics by GRETCHEN CRYER
Music by NANCY FORD

6 men, 4 women—Bare stage

This new musical by the authors of *The Last Sweet Days of Isaac* was a hit at Joseph Papp's Public Theatre and transferred to the Circle-in-the-Square theatre in New York for a successful off-Broadway run. It is about a 40-year-old song writer who wants to make a come-back. The central conflict is between the song writer and her manager. She wants to include feminist material in her act—he wants her to go back to the syrupy-sweet, non-controversial formula which was once successful. "Clearly the most imaginative and melodic score heard in New York all season."—Soho Weekly News. "Brash, funny, very agreeable in its brash and funny way, and moreover, it touches a special emotional chord for our times."—N.Y. Post.   (#11025)

ON THE TWENTIETH CENTURY
(ALL GROUPS—MUSICAL COMEDY)

Book and Lyrics by ADOLPH GREEN and BETTY COMDEN, Music by CY COLEMAN

17 principal roles, plus singers and extras (doubling possible)—Various sets

Whether performed with elaborate scenery, or on a simple skeletal scale, this brilliantly comic musical can appeal to audiences everywhere. This is truly an extravagant show—but its extravagance lies not in its scenery and physical production, but in the boisterous, tumultuous energy—and in the lush and sprightly energetic surge of its very melodic score. The story concerns the efforts of a flamboyant theatrical impressario to persuade a film star to appear in his next production, to outwit rival producers and creditors, to rid himself of religious nut Letitia Primrose (played by Imogene Coca on Broadway) and Lily's film star boyfriend Bruce Granit (who's as strong in profile as he is weak in brains). And, he must do all this before the famed 20th Century Ltd. reaches NYC! The story, and it's two leading characters—the mad impressario Oscar Jaffe and the love of his life and his greatest star Lily Garland—can be loved and enjoyed by all audiences. "Spectacular . . . funny . . . elegant . . . civilized wit and wild humor."—N.Y. Times. "A perfect musical . . . a gorgeous show!"—N.Y. Post.　　　　　　　(#819)

KURT VONNEGUT'S GOD BLESS YOU, MR. ROSEWATER
(MUSICAL SATIRE)
By the creators of LITTLE SHOP OF HORRORS

Book and Lyrics by HOWARD ASHMAN
Music by ALAN MENKEN
Additional lyrics by DENNIS GREEN

10 men, 4 women (principals—also double smaller roles), extras, musicians—Various interiors and exteriors

"One of Vonnegut's most affecting and likeable novels becomes an affecting and likable theatrical experience, with more inventiveness, cockeyed characters, high-muzzle-velocity dialogue and just plain energy that you get from the majority of play-wrights."—Newsweek. Eliot Rosewater's a well-intentioned idealist and philanthropic nut—and as president of a multi-million family foundation dispenses money to arcane and artsy-crafty projects. He's also a World War II veteran with a guilt complex, haunted by all this wealth—and also slightly crazy. His outlandish behavior enrages his senator dad, alienates his society-conscious wife—and the money attracts a young, shyster lawyer who tries to divert it to an obscure branch of the family. It portrays Vonnegut's vision of money, avarice and human behavior—as it aims a satirical fusillade at plastic America, fast foods, trademarks, slogans, media blitzes and the follies of materialism. "A charming, delightful, unexpected and thoughtful musical."—N.Y. Post.　　　　(#630)

Other Publications for Your Interest

PUMP BOYS AND DINETTES
(ALL GROUPS—MUSICAL)
By JOHN FOLEY, MARK HARDWICK, DEBRA MONK, CASS MORGAN, JOHN SCHIMMEL and JIM WANN

4 men, 2 women—Composite Interior

This delightful little show went from Off Off Broadway to Off Broadway to Broadway, where it had a long run. This is an evening of country/western songs performed by the actors—on guitars, piano, bass and, yes, kitchen utensils. There are the four Pump Boys: L.M. on the Piano (singing such delights as "The Night Dolly Parton Was Almost Mine"), Jim on rhythm guitar (the spokesman of the Pump Boys), Jackson on lead guitar (whose rocker about Mona, a check-out girl at Woolworth's, stops the show) and Eddie, who plays bass. The Dinettes are Prudie and Rhetta Cupp, who run the Double Cupp Diner across from the Pump Boys' gas station. "Totally delightful . . . the easiest, chummiest, happiest show in town."—Newsweek. "Totally terrific."—N.Y. Post. "It tickles the funny bone and makes everybody feel, just for the evening, like a good ole boy or a good ole girl."—Time. "It doesn't merely celebrate the value of friendship and life's simple pleasures, it embodies them."—N.Y. Times.   (#18135)

GOLD DUST
(ALL GROUPS—MUSICAL)
Book by JON JORY
Music and Lyrics by JIM WANN

5 men, 3 women, 3 piece combo—Interior

Set in a saloon in a western mining camp in the 1850's, *Gold Dust* is a *very* loose musical adaptation of Molière's *The Miser*. The story concerns a prospector named Jebediah Harp who has hit it rich and hoards his gold. Perfect for high schools, colleges and community theatres, this is another hit from Louisville's famed Actors Theater. The music and lyrics are by the very talented Jim Wann, whose other works include *Pump Boys and Dinettes*, *Diamond Studs* and *Hot Grog*. "It's spunky and raucous, clangorous and tuneful. It overflows with a theatrical zest that is pretty much irresistible."—Louisville Courier Journal. ". . . the small musical that budget-minded theatres across the land have been praying for."—Louisville Times. "Best of all is Wann's music, a mixture of jazz, blues, rock, folk and country-western styles."—Variety.   (#9134)

FAVORITE MUSICALS *from*

"The House of Plays"

A FINE AND PRIVATE PLACE

(All Groups) Book & Lyrics by Erik Haagensen. Music by Richard Isen. Adapted from the novel by Peter S. Beagle. 3m., 2f, (may be played by 2m., 2f.) + 1 raven (may be either m. or f.) Ext. setting. "The grave's a fine and private place,/But none, I think, do there embrace." Little did you know, Andrew Marvell, that someday, someone would come up with a charming love story, set in a graveyard, about two lost souls who are buried there, who meet and fall in love. Also inhabiting the cemetery is an eccentric old man who has the gift of being able to see and converse with the inhabitants of the graves, as well as with a raven who swoops in at mealtimes with some dinner he has swiped for the old guy. Also present from time to time is a delightful old Jewish widow, whose husband Morris is buried in the cemetery. She often stops by to tell Morris what's new. Her name is Gertrude, and it is soon apparent that she also stops by to flirt with old Jonathan Rebeck (she doesn't know he actually *lives* there). A crisis arises when it appears the young couple will be separated. The young man, it seems, has been deemed a suicide and, as such, he must be removed from consecrated ground. Their only hope is Jonathan; but to help them Jonathan must come out in the open. Had we but world enough, and time, we would tell you how Jonathan manages to salvage the romance; but we'll just have to hope the above story intrigues you enough to examine the delightful libretto and wonderfully tuneful music for yourself. A sell-out, smash hit at the Goodspeed in Connecticut and, later, at the American Stage Co. in New Jersey (the professional theatre which premiered *Other People's Money)*, this happy, whimsical, sentimental, up-beat new show will delight audiences of all ages. .   **(#8154)**